ARLENE FELTMAN SAILHAC'S
DE GUSTIBUS GREAT COOKS' COOKBOOKS

Mediterranean Cooking

ARLENE FELTMAN SAILHAC'S
DE GUSTIBUS GREAT COOKS' COOKBOOKS

Mediterranean Cooking

PHOTOGRAPHS BY TOM ECKERLE
DESIGN BY MARTIN LUBIN

BLACK DOG & LEVENTHAL
NEW YORK

Published by

Black Dog & Leventhal Publishers, Inc.

151 West 19th Street
New York, NY 10011

Distributed by

Workman Publishing Company

708 Broadway
New York, NY 10003

Manufactured in Hong Kong

ISBN: 1-884822-33-9

h g f e d c b a

DEDICATION

I dedicate this book to my family, which loves to eat:

My parents, Adelaide and Stanley Kessler

My sister, brother-in-law, and niece, Gayle, Stanley, and Amy Miller

My Grandma Berdie, who opened my eyes to food

And to Alain Sailhac and Todd Feltman, the two "men in my life who are my favorite dining partners."

ACKNOWLEDGMENTS

During the fifteen-year existence of De Gustibus at Macy's, many people have given their support and encouragment.

First, my profound thanks to all the wonderful chefs and cooks who have taught at De Gustibus at Macy's. A special thanks to: Colman Andrews, Terrance Brennan, Charles Bowman, Dominick Cerrone, Andew D'Amico, Gary Danko, Alain Ducasse, Todd English, Bobby Flay, Joyce Goldstein, Matthew Kenney, Thomas Valenti, and Paula Wolfert.

Thanks to my priceless assistants who are always there for me in a million ways: Jane Asche, Barbara Bjorn, Pam Carey, Corinne Gherardi, Yonina Jacobs, Nancy Robbins, and Betti Zucker.

Thanks to Barbara Teplitz for all her help and support throughout the years, and to Gertrud Yampierre for holding the office together.

Thanks to Ruth Schwartz for believing in the concept of De Gustibus and helping to orchestrate its initiation at Macy's.

Thanks to everyone at Macy's Herald Square who have supported De Gustibus at Macy's since its inception, with special notice to the Public Relations and Advertising Departments who helped spread the word.

Thanks to J.P. Leventhal and Pamela Horn of Black Dog & Leventhal Publishers for providing the vehicle to put our cooking classes into book form and for being so encouraging.

A special thanks to Jane Asche for her help in the beginning stages of the book.

Thanks to Tom Eckerle for his magical photographs; Ceci Gallini for her impeccable taste and prop design; and Roscoe Betsill, whose food styling really took this project to another level.

Thanks for supplying the exquisite props for the photographs to Pottery Barn and Cobweb in New York City.

Thanks to Marty Lubin for his wonderful design.

Thanks to Mary Goodbody and Judith Sutton for making the book "user friendly."

Thanks to my agent Judith Weber for her help and advice.

Special thanks to Judith Choate, who shaped all my words into meaningful prose and never ceased to amaze me with her knowledge of food and her patience and calm, and to Steve Pool for getting these words into the computer with smiles and enthusiasm.

Heartfelt thanks to the entire Kobrand Corporation, purveyors of fine wine, especially Cathleen Burke and Kimberly Charles for opening the door for the marriage of fine wine and great food for the last ten years.

Finally, thanks to all the faithful De Gustibus customers who have made all our classes spring to life.

Contents

Foreword

Fifteen years ago, the popularity of cooking classes was growing all over the United States. While interest was high, New Yorkers could not always fit an ongoing series of classes into their busy schedules. Demonstration classes seemed to me to be the answer, and De Gustibus was born. What began as four chefs and an electric frying pan on a stage developed into over 350 chefs and cooking teachers demonstrating their specialties in a professionally equipped kitchen for groups of fervent food-lovers.

When we started De Gustibus in 1980, we had no inkling of the variety of new cuisines that would become an integral part of American cooking. Since then, we have discovered New World Cuisine, Florida Cuisine, Light Cooking, Fusion Cooking, Cajun Cooking, Southwest Cooking—you name it! As American and international cuisines have changed and our tastes have broadened, De Gustibus has stayed on the cutting edge of the culinary experience. We have invited teachers, cooks, and chefs to De Gustibus both because of their level of recognition in the food world and because of their challenging, unique, current, and, above all, noteworthy cooking styles.

The goal of the cooking demonstrations at De Gustibus is to make the art of the grand master chefs and cooks accessible for the home kitchen. Each chef leads the way and holds out a helping hand to the home cook. The results depend as much on the cook's wit, self-confidence, and interest as they do on a great recipe. Thus, students, and now readers of this book, can learn to master the recipes of the most sophisticated chefs and cooks.

The reason De Gustibus demonstration classes are so popular is that they allow the novice the opportunity to feel the passion—as well as to see each professional chef's or cook's technique, order, and discipline. By seeing how each chef's personality influences the final product, serious home cooks gain the confidence to trust their own tastes and instincts. New and unfamiliar ingredients, untried techniques, and even a little dazzle all find a place in the amateur's kitchen.

This book introduces some of the best and most popular menus demonstrated throughout the years. Each dish is designed to serve six people, unless otherwise noted. All the menus were prepared in class, and I have done little to alter them other than to test and streamline recipes for the home kitchen. I have also provided each chef's strategy and Kobrand Distributors' wine suggestions with every menu.

ARLENE FELTMAN SAILHAC
1996

Introduction

Mediterranean Cooking sings with the flavors of leisurely meals redolent of aromatic herbs and subtle spices. It is filled with wondrous recipes that make us dream longingly of southern France, Italy, Spain, Greece, Turkey, the Middle East, and North Africa: regions of the world drenched in sun and touched by turquoise waters. Olives of many hues and flavors, juicy, sweet tomatoes, pungent garlic, deeply flavored grains, dense golden honeys, fragrant herbs, bountiful fruit, and creamy cheeses; the tastes dance in our heads as images of the countries represented here evoke a more tranquil way of life. Conjuring up faraway spots and ancient times, chefs have filled the De Gustibus classroom with the spirit of these magical places.

Even though the Mediterranean countries are far away, the ingredients used to create the numerous cuisines of this enchanting region are not foreign to the American palate. Purchased from an impersonal supermarket, they may not taste as they do when gathered in the country or bartered for in farmers' markets, but they are readily available to us in all their versatility. This means that the recipes featured on these pages can easily be recreated in the home kitchen.

The food experts and cooks who have brought the techniques and flavors of these provincial cuisines to the De Gustibus kitchen have ranged from those who hold them inviolate to bold young American chefs who use them as a springboard for experimentation. Paula Wolfert and Colman Andrews rely on a zest for adventure to lead them to authentic recipes, fine home cooks, and kitchen traditions, all of which they report on in their indigenous forms. Innovative chefs such as Andrew D'Amico and Terrance Brennan expand on traditional recipes and combine their ingredients in unexpected ways to create new dishes that are fearless in accomplishment and seductive in flavor. These proponents offer the food as it suits their style of cooking—and we benefit greatly, from both positions.

We recognize that even the most serious home cook does not have a battery of helpers waiting to chop, mince, stir, wash, and clean. Food purveyors do not deliver ingredients and provisions to the back door, and stocks and sauces do not simmer all day on the back burner. This, however, does not mean the serious home cook cannot prepare a meal worthy of four stars if he or she learns what every professional knows: Organize! Prepare! Taste! And, above all, trust yourself and don't be intimidated by tradition.

The cuisines of the Mediterranean are, for the most part, rustic in execution and audacious in flavor: a perfect canvas on which home cooks can expand their repertoire. Colorful ingredients, eye-catching textures, and mouth-watering taste sensations all combine for foods that are intensely flavorful and quite easy to prepare. Bask in the sun of the creative chefs we have featured at De Gustibus as they lead us on a culinary cruise through the romance of the Mediterranean.

STRATEGIES FOR COOKING FROM OUR GREAT CHEFS AND COOKS

Before beginning to prepare any meal, regardless of how simple or how complicated, take the following steps to heart:

1 Read through the entire menu and its recipes in advance.

2 Complete as many recipes, or steps, as possible ahead of time, taking care to allow time for defrosting, reheating, bringing to room temperature, or whatever the recipe requires before serving.

For each menu, we provide a feature entitled "What You Can Prepare Ahead of Time." This offers timesaving hints for the cook who is preparing the entire menu, or elements of it, and wants to do much of the preparation before the

actual day of the meal. While many foods taste better fresh rather than reheated, we include these lists for your convenience, as suggestions only—not as required do-ahead instructions.

3 Place all the ingredients for a particular recipe on, or in, individual trays, plates, or bowls according to the specific steps in the recipe. Each item should be washed, chopped, measured, separated—or whatever is called for—before you begin to cook. This organizational technique, known as the *mise en place* (from the French, it literally means "putting in place"), is the most valuable lesson we at De Gustibus have learned from the pros. We strongly urge you to cook this way.

Note that when a recipe calls for a particular ingredient to be cut in a certain size or shape, it matters. The final result is often dependent upon the textures and colors, as well as the flavor, of the ingredients.

4 Use only the best ingredients available. All good chefs and cooks stress this. Try to find the exact ingredient called for, but if you cannot, substitute as suggested in the recipe or glossary, or use your common sense.

5 Rely on your taste buds. They will not lie!

6 Clean up as you work.

Use the following menu suggestions in full, or plan meals around one or two elements from a menu. Educate yourself, and have fun with new ingredients and flavors.

Mise en place tray

The Cooks

Colman Andrews
Food Writer; Executive Editor, *Saveur Magazine*, New York, New York
Author: *Catalan Cuisine, Everything on the Table*

Gary Danko
Executive Chef, The Dining Room at the Ritz-Carlton Hotel, San Francisco, California

Matthew Kenney
Chef / Owner, Matthew's Restaurant *and* Bar Anise, New York, New York

Charles Bowman
Chef, Periyali, New York, New York

Alain Ducasse
Executive Chef, Restaurant Le Louis XV, Monte Carlo, Monaco

Thomas Valenti
Executive Chef / Co-Owner, Cascabel, New York, New York

Terrance Brennan
Executive Chef/Owner, Picholine, New York, New York

Todd English
Chef / Owner, Olives *and* Figs, Charleston, Massachusetts

Paula Wolfert
Food Writer, San Francisco, California
Author: *The Cooking of the Eastern Mediterranean, Paula Wolfert's World of Food, The Cooking of Southwest France, Couscous and Other Good Foods from Morocco*

Dominick Cerrone
Executive Chef / Owner, Solera, New York, New York

Bobby Flay
Executive Chef / Co-Owner, Mesa Grill *and* Bolo, New York, New York
Author: *Bold American Food*

Andrew D'Amico
Executive Chef / Partner, The Sign of the Dove, New York, New York

Joyce Goldstein
Chef / Owner, Square One, San Francisco, California
Author: *Mediterranean the Beautiful, Back to Square One, The Mediterranean Kitchen*

Techniques

CUTTING VEGETABLES

Into julienne: Using a small, very sharp knife, a mandoline, or an inexpensive vegetable slicer, cut vegetables into thin, uniform sticks, usually about ¼ inch thick and 1 to 2 inches long.

Into dice: Trim vegetables into uniform rectangles. Using a very sharp knife, cut into strips ranging in width from ⅛ to ¼ inch, depending upon the size dice you require. Lay the strips together and cut into even dice by crosscutting into squares ⅛ to ¼ inch across.

BLANCHING VEGETABLES

Place trimmed vegetables (or fruit) into rapidly boiling water for a brief period, often no more than 30 seconds, then immediately drain and plunge into ice cold water to stop the cooking process.

CLARIFYING BUTTER

Clarified butter burns less easily and keeps longer than regular butter.

CLARIFIED BUTTER
MAKES ABOUT 3 CUPS

2 pounds unsalted butter, cut into pieces

1 Melt the butter in a medium-sized saucepan over very low heat. Skim off the foam that rises to the top using a ladle, taking care to remove as little of the clear yellow fat as possible.

2 Let the butter cool slightly and settle. Carefully strain the butter through a fine sieve into a clean glass container, leaving the milky residue on the bottom of the saucepan. Discard the residue.

3 Cover and refrigerate for up to 2 weeks or freeze for up to 1 month.

ROASTING PEPPERS

Using a fork with a heat-proof handle, hold a pepper over a gas burner, without actually placing the pepper in the flame, until the skin puffs and is charred black. Turn as necessary to ensure that the entire pepper is charred. Place the charred pepper in a plastic bag, seal, and steam for about 10 minutes.

Remove the pepper from the bag and pull off the charred skin. Stem and seed. Dice, chop, or purée.

If using an electric stove, place the pepper in a large dry cast-iron skillet over medium-high heat. Cook slowly, turning frequently, until completely charred. Proceed as above.

To roast several peppers, place them on a sheet pan under a preheated broiler. Position as close to the heat as possible without touching the flame or coil and roast until the skin puffs and is charred black. Turn to char the entire peppers. Proceed as described above.

ROASTING GARLIC

You can roast whole garlic bulbs or you can separate into individual cloves.

ROASTED GARLIC

1 or more whole garlic bulbs (heads) or 1 or more cloves garlic

1 Preheat the oven to 200 degrees F.

2 Loosely wrap the garlic in aluminum foil. Place on a small baking sheet. Bake for about 1 hour for a whole bulb or 15 minutes for individual cloves, or until the pulp is very soft. Remove from the oven. Unwrap and allow to cool.

For whole bulbs: Cut in half crosswise. Working from the closed ends, gently push the pulp from the skin. Discard the skin.

For individual cloves: Slit the skin using the point of a sharp knife. Peel, or gently push the pulp from the skin. Discard the skin.

TOASTING SPICES AND SEEDS

Toast spices and seeds in a heavy cast-iron skillet over medium heat, stirring or shaking the pan frequently. Toast for 2 to 5 minutes, depending on the ingredient, or until it turns a shade darker and is fragrant.

PITTING OLIVES

Place olives between two kitchen towels and pound gently with a mallet or the broad side of a cleaver. Unwrap and remove the pits from the flesh.

TOASTING AND SKINNING NUTS

Preheat the oven to 400 degrees F. Spread the nuts in a single layer on a baking sheet. Using a spray bottle, lightly spray the nuts with water. Roast for 5 to 10 minutes, depending on the nut's size and oil content, or until golden. Immediately remove from the oven and transfer to a plate or tray to cool. If the nuts have skins, the steam created in the oven will usually cause the skins to slip right off. If not, spread the hot nuts on a kitchen towel and cool slightly, then wrap them in the towel and rub back and forth to remove the skins.

To skin only, blanch nuts in boiling water for 1 minute. Drain, place in a kitchen towel, and rub back and forth to remove the skins.

Pantry Recipes

We supply standard recipes for the chicken, veal, fish, and vegetable stocks used in the recipes. Homemade stock adds a depth of flavor to a dish not possible with canned broth. If time is a factor, use low-sodium canned broth.

CHICKEN STOCK
MAKES ABOUT 4 CUPS
PREPARATION TIME: ABOUT 40 MINUTES
COOKING TIME: ABOUT 2 HOURS AND 30 MINUTES

2 quarts (8 cups) water
2 chicken carcasses, chopped into small pieces
3 onions, chopped
1 carrot, chopped
2 ribs celery, chopped
3 sprigs fresh thyme
3 sprigs fresh parsley
1 bay leaf
1 tablespoon white peppercorns

1 In a stockpot or large saucepan, combine the water and chopped carcasses. Bring to a simmer over medium heat and skim the surface of any foam.

2 Add the onions, carrots, celery, thyme, parsley, bay leaf, and peppercorns. Bring to a boil, reduce the heat, and simmer for 1½ to 2 hours, skimming fat and foam from the surface as necessary, until reduced to 4 cups.

3 Pour the stock through a fine sieve into a clean pan and press against the solids to extract as much liquid as possible. Discard the solids. Cool to tepid (this can be done by plunging the pan into a sinkful of ice), cover, and refrigerate for 6 hours, or until the fat particles have risen to the top. Spoon off the solidified fat and discard.

4 Bring the stock to a simmer over medium-high heat and simmer for about 30 minutes. Adjust the seasonings and use as directed in the recipe.

5 To store, cool to tepid, cover, and refrigerate for 2 to 3 days or freeze in 1-cup quantities (for ease of use) for up to 3 months.

VEAL STOCK
MAKES ABOUT 3 QUARTS
PREPARATION TIME: ABOUT 40 MINUTES
COOKING TIME: ABOUT 7 HOURS

¼ cup plus 2 tablespoons vegetable oil
4 pounds veal marrow bones, chopped into 2-inch pieces
3 onions, quartered
1 carrot, chopped
1 rib celery, chopped
1 tomato, quartered
1 bay leaf
1 tablespoon black peppercorns
2 sprigs fresh thyme
3 cloves garlic, crushed
Approximately 4 quarts (16 cups) water

1 Preheat the oven to 450 degrees F.

2 Using ¼ cup of the oil, lightly oil the bones. Spread the bones in a single layer in a large roasting pan. Roast, turning occasionally, for 20 minutes, or until the bones are dark golden brown on all sides.

3 Transfer the bones to a stockpot or large saucepan. Add the remaining 2 tablespoons oil to the roasting pan and stir in the onions, carrots, celery, and tomatoes. Cook on top of the stove over medium-high heat, stirring frequently, for about 15 minutes, until well browned.

4 With a slotted spoon, transfer the vegetables to the stockpot. Add the bay leaf, peppercorns, thyme, and garlic.

5 Pour off the fat from the roasting pan and discard. Set the pan over medium heat and deglaze it with 2 cups of water, scraping up any particles sticking to the bottom. Add this liquid to the stockpot. Add enough water to the stockpot to cover the bones by 2 inches and bring to a boil. Reduce the heat and let the stock barely simmer, uncovered, for 6 hours, skimming fat and foam from the surface as necessary. Remove from the heat. Cool (this can be done by plunging the stockpot into a sinkful of ice), cover, and refrigerate for 12 hours or overnight.

6 Spoon the fat from the surface of the stock and pour the stock through a fine sieve into a clean pan. Spoon off any remaining trace of fat. Place the pan over high heat and bring to a rolling boil. Reduce the heat and simmer for 30 minutes, or until the flavor is full-bodied and the stock has reduced slightly. Use as directed in the recipe.

7 To store, cool to tepid, cover, and refrigerate for 2 to 3 days or freeze in 1-cup quantities (for ease of use) for up to 3 months.

FISH STOCK
MAKES ABOUT 3 CUPS
PREPARATION TIME: ABOUT 20 MINUTES
COOKING TIME: ABOUT 25 MINUTES

If you have no time to make stock, substitute bottled clam broth or low-sodium chicken broth.

2 sprigs fresh parsley
2 sprigs fresh thyme
1 small bay leaf
2 pounds fish bones (from saltwater fish such as sole, John Dory, turbot, halibut, or other very fresh, nonoily fish), chopped into pieces
2 tablespoons canola or other flavorless oil
1 small onion, chopped
1 rib celery, chopped
1 cup dry white wine

1 Using kitchen twine, make a *bouquet garni* by tying the parsley, thyme, and bay leaf together. Set aside.

2 Rinse the fish bones under cold running water.

3 In a large saucepan or stockpot, heat the oil over medium heat. Add the fish bones and vegetables. Reduce the heat and lay a piece of wax paper directly on the bones and vegetables. Cook for 10 minutes, stirring once or twice to prevent browning. (Be careful not to push the paper into the pan.)

4 Remove the wax paper. Add the wine and enough water to cover the bones and vegetables by about 2 inches. Add the *bouquet garni*. Raise the heat to high and bring to a boil. Skim the surface of all foam. Reduce the heat and simmer for 20 to 25 minutes.

5 Strain the stock through an extra-fine sieve into a clean pan. Discard the solids. Use as directed in the recipe.

6 To store, cool to tepid (this can be done by plunging the pan into a sinkful of ice), cover, and refrigerate for 2 to 3 days or freeze in 1-cup quantities (for ease of use) for up to 3 weeks.

VEGETABLE STOCK
MAKES ABOUT 3 CUPS
PREPARATION TIME: ABOUT 20 MINUTES
COOKING TIME: ABOUT 2 HOURS

If you do not have the time to make stock, substitute a low-sodium vegetable broth.

3 quarts cold water
1 carrot, chopped
1 potato, peeled and chopped
1 large onion, chopped
3 ribs celery, chopped
1/2 leek, white part only, chopped
1 small tomato, chopped
1 tablespoon salt, or to taste
2 cloves garlic, peeled
1 teaspoon chopped fresh flat-leaf parsley
1/2 teaspoon black peppercorns

1 In a large saucepan, bring 1 cup of the water to a boil over medium-high heat. Add the carrots, potatoes, onions, celery, leeks, tomatoes, and salt. Cook for 5 minutes, stirring occasionally.

2 Add the remaining 11 cups water to the pan, along with the garlic, parsley, and peppercorns. Bring to a simmer, reduce the heat to low, and simmer gently for 2 hours.

3 Strain the liquid through a fine sieve into a bowl. Cool for about 1 hour and then pour the stock through a fine sieve again. Use as directed in the recipe.

4 To store, cover and refrigerate for up to 3 days or freeze in 1-cup quantities (for ease of use) for up to 3 months.

A SPANISH REPAST

Catalan Tomato Bread
PA AMB TOMAQUET

Swordfish with Pine Nuts and Raisins
PEIX ESPASA EN CASSOLA

Banana Fritters
TORTITAS DE PLATANOS

Champagne *(first course)*
Rioja or Rias Baixas *(second course)*
Dry Rosé such as Tavel *(dessert)*

WHAT YOU CAN PREPARE AHEAD OF TIME

Early in the day: Soak and drain the anchovies for the Catalan Tomato Bread. Toast the bread for the same recipe. Prepare the ingredients for the Swordfish with Pine Nuts and Raisins. Pulverize the almonds for the swordfish.

Up to 3 hours ahead: Make the Banana Fritters.

Colman Andrews is one of America's most distinguished food writers. When he introduced himself to the De Gustibus classroom he said, "I am not a chef, just a lover of the foods of Catalan. I want to share with you the ingredients and cooking methods of this ancient land, which has been influenced as much by its geographical proximity to the Mediterranean as by its roots in Spain." He proceeded to demonstrate that although we might all be familiar with the basic ingredients, such as tomatoes, garlic, parsley, pine nuts, raisins, and wonderfully fresh fish, the Catalans use them by giving them a different twist. The ease with which he prepared these recipes made this almost undiscovered cuisine deliciously inviting and exciting to the students.

◁ COLMAN ANDREWS: *Ingredients for Catalan Tomato Bread*

Catalan Tomato Bread

Pa amb Tomaquet

This simple combination of country-style bread and lush, ripe tomatoes is a fantastic introduction to casual Mediterranean dining. For a relaxed meal *al fresco*, you might want to place all the ingredients on the table and let your guests assemble their own plates. Colman told us that ham, sardines, herring, or sausage are all welcome additions.

24 large anchovy fillets
Six 1½-inch-thick slices country-style French or Italian bread (see Note)
3 medium-sized very ripe tomatoes, halved
About ½ cup mild Spanish extra-virgin olive oil (preferably a Catalan brand, such as Siurana, Verge de Borges, or Lerida)
Salt to taste

1 Assemble *mise en place* trays for this recipe (see page 7).

2 Place the anchovy fillets in a small bowl and add enough cool water to cover. Allow to soak for 1 hour. Drain and pat dry.

3 Prepare a charcoal or gas grill or preheat the broiler.

4 Lightly toast the bread on both sides over the fire or under the broiler.

5 Squeezing gently, rub the tomatoes over both sides of each slice of toast, leaving a thin film of tomato flesh and seeds on the surfaces. Drizzle olive oil to taste evenly over both sides of each toast. Sprinkle both sides with salt to taste. Place 1 toast slice on each plate. Arrange 4 anchovy fillets on top of each toast and serve immediately.

NOTE: You will need a large round or oval dense hearty bread. Do not use a baguette, as it will not be of the right consistency to absorb the tomato juices and oil properly.

COLMAN ANDREWS:
Catalan Tomato Bread

Swordfish with Pine Nuts and Raisins

Peix Espasa en Cassola

Relying on an unusual combination of sweet and sour flavors, Colman has created a unique way to cook fish. The sauce works equally well with chicken breasts.

2 pounds swordfish, about 1 inch thick, cut into 2 x 3-inch pieces
1/4 cup all-purpose flour
2 tablespoons Spanish olive oil
1 1/2 cups dry white wine
3/4 cup fresh orange juice
1 1/2 tablespoons fresh lemon juice
24 toasted blanched almonds
2 sprigs fresh flat-leaf parsley, minced
2 sprigs fresh mint, leaves only, minced
2 sprigs fresh marjoram or oregano, leaves only, minced
1/2 cup golden raisins, plumped in water and drained
1/2 cup toasted pine nuts
Coarse salt and freshly ground black pepper to taste

1 Assemble *mise en place* trays for this recipe (see page 7).

2 Dredge the swordfish pieces in the flour. In a large non-stick skillet, heat the oil over medium heat. Add the fish and cook for about 5 minutes, or until lightly browned on all sides. Drain on paper towels and set aside.

3 Return the skillet to the heat, add the wine and citrus juices, bring to a boil, and boil, stirring frequently, for about 15 minutes, or until the liquid is reduced to 3/4 cup.

4 While the liquid is reducing, pulverize the almonds in a mortar and pestle. Add the herbs and about 1 tablespoon of the reducing liquid and work into the almonds to form a thick paste. This is called a *picada*.

5 Add the raisins, pine nuts, and *picada* to the skillet and stir to combine. Return the fish to the skillet and cook, stirring gently, for about 3 minutes, or until the fish is hot and opaque throughout and the flavors are well blended. Season to taste with coarse salt and pepper. Serve immediately, with rice or a green salad if desired.

NOTE: Unless you use a mortar and pestle to pulverize the almonds, the sauce will be chunky rather than smooth. If you don't have one, use a food processor fitted with the metal blade and pulse just until the nuts are smooth, taking care not to overprocess them.

COLMAN ANDREWS: *Swordfish with Pine Nuts and Raisins*

Banana Fritters

Tortitas de Platanos

These simple doughnut-like treats are easy to make and always draw raves. They are also a marvelous way to use overripe bananas. What's more, you can make them several hours before serving.

1 pound very ripe bananas, peeled and mashed
6 large eggs
1/2 cup milk
2 to 3 tablespoons dark rum, or to taste
Grated zest of 1 lemon
1/2 teaspoon ground cinnamon
Pinch of salt
1 teaspoon active dry yeast
3 to 4 cups all-purpose flour
4 cups corn oil
4 large pieces orange peel
About 1/2 cup confectioners' sugar

1 Assemble *mise en place* trays for this recipe (see page 7).

2 In a bowl, combine the bananas and eggs. Add the milk, rum, lemon zest, cinnamon, and salt and whisk until well blended. Add the yeast, whisking, then add just enough flour to make a smooth batter that is the consistency of softly whipped cream. Cover and set aside to rest for 30 minutes.

3 In a large heavy nonstick frying pan, heat the oil over medium-high heat until hot (see Note). Add the orange peel and cook for about 2 minutes, or until the peel begins to brown. Remove and discard the peel, and heat the oil until it registers 360 degrees F on a candy thermometer. Use a soup spoon to form the batter into small ovals, drop the ovals into the oil, a few at a time, and fry for about 3 minutes, or until golden and crisp. Using a slotted spoon, remove the fritters and drain on paper towels. Continue until all the batter has been used.

4 Using a fine sieve or sugar shaker, lightly dust the warm fritters with confectioners' sugar. Serve warm or at room temperature.

NOTE: The oil must be deep enough for the fritters to float freely, or they will brown too quickly and still be raw in the center.

◁ COLMAN ANDREWS: *Banana Fritters*

A TASTE OF GREECE

Spanakopita

Almond Skordalia

White Beans with Garlic

Fillet of Snapper with Tomato, Onion, and Garlic

Baklava

WINE SUGGESTIONS:

Sparkling Wine, Champagne, or Greek White Wine such as
Mantinia or Anhialos *(first course)*
Sauvignon Blanc or Pinot Blanc *(second course)*
Muscat de Patras (Greek dessert wine) or Tawny Port *(dessert)*

WHAT YOU CAN PREPARE AHEAD OF TIME

Up to 1 week ahead: Prepare and freeze the Spanakopita. (See recipe note.) Make the Clarified Butter.

Up to 2 days ahead: Make the Skordalia and White Beans with Garlic.

Up to 1 day ahead: Prepare the tomato sauce for the Fillet of Snapper. Cover and refrigerate. Prepare the Baklava. Cover and store at room temperature.

Charles Bowman came to De Gustibus on the wave of the popularity of the New York City restaurant, Periyali, owned by Nicola Kotsoni and Steve Tzolis. Although he had worked with Charles Palmer at the very American River Café in Brooklyn, he had always had a special love for Greek food. His enthusiasm and knowledge helped the Greek owners of Periyali create a fine restaurant featuring classic Greek cooking tempered by memories of their mothers' kitchens. For his class, Charles prepared a plate of typical *meze*, tempting appetizers that form a complete meal when served with his signature fillet of snapper.

◁ CHARLES BOWMAN: *Spanakopita, Almond Skordalia,* and *White Beans with Garlic*

Spanakopita

This crispy spinach-filled appetizer can be made well in advance, frozen, and then reheated.

½ cup plus 1 tablespoon extra-virgin olive oil
½ cup shredded onions
½ cup shredded leeks
Three 10-ounce packages frozen chopped spinach, thawed, drained, and squeezed of all excess liquid
2 tablespoons chopped fresh dill
1 teaspoon salt, or to taste
¼ teaspoon freshly ground white pepper
2 large eggs
¾ cup crumbled feta cheese
¼ cup small-curd cottage cheese
1 tablespoon freshly grated Parmesan cheese
1 tablespoon dry bread crumbs
20 sheets phyllo dough, thawed according to the package directions
2 cups Clarified Butter (see page 9), melted

■ Special Equipment: Pizza cutter (optional)

1 Assemble *mise en place* trays for this recipe (see page 7).

2 In a large skillet, heat 1 tablespoon of the oil over medium heat. Add the onions and leeks and sauté for about 5 minutes, or until lightly browned. Stir in the spinach and the remaining ½ cup oil and cook, stirring constantly, for about 4 minutes. Add the dill, salt, and white pepper and stir to blend. Transfer to a large bowl. Cover and refrigerate for 1 hour, or until well chilled.

3 Preheat the oven to 400 degrees F.

4 Stir the eggs, cheeses, and bread crumbs into the spinach mixture. Set aside.

5 Lay the phyllo sheets on a dry work surface with a long side toward you. Using a ruler and a pizza cutter or a very sharp knife, cut the sheets crosswise into three 5½-inch-wide strips. Lift off 12 strips and fold crosswise in half. Cut at the fold to make 24 pieces. Again fold the strips in half and cut to make 48 pieces in all. Set aside, covered with a well-wrung-out damp kitchen towel. These will be used as patches to reinforce the phyllo under the filling.

6 Lay 2 strips of dough side by side on the work surface.

(Keep the strips that you are not actually working with covered with a well-wrung-out damp kitchen towel so that the pastry doesn't dry out.) Using a pastry brush, lightly and completely coat both strips with clarified butter, starting at the center and working out toward the ends. Position a phyllo patch lengthwise about an inch up from the bottom and in the center of each strip. Butter the patches.

7 Working quickly, place 1 rounded measuring teaspoon of the filling in the center of 1 patch. Fold the sides of the strip over the filling. Brush the folds with clarified butter. Fold the bottom of the strip up over the filling to form a triangular point, then continue folding, making sure that with each fold you align the bottom edge with the alternate side of the pastry strip, as if you were folding a flag. Lightly coat the finished triangle with butter and place on an ungreased baking sheet. Repeat with the second strip, then continue until all of the phyllo is used.

8 Bake in the top third of the oven for 10 minutes. Brush the triangles with butter again and continue to bake for 10 to 15 minutes longer, or until golden brown. Cool slightly on wire racks and serve warm or at room temperature.

ALTERNATIVE TECHNIQUE: To create Spanakopita rolls, complete the instructions through step 6. Then place 1 rounded measuring teaspoon of the filling in the center of 1 patch. Beginning at the short end, roll the phyllo into a roll to encase the filling. Brush the end of the strip with clarified butter and press to seal the roll. Continue with the instructions in step 7. Instead of folding the strip, roll it up to encase the filling, lightly coating the finished rolls and placing on the baking sheet. Proceed with step 8.

NOTE: If the triangles will be eaten within an hour or so, you can reheat them in a 375-degree-F oven for 10 minutes, or microwave on high for 30 seconds. The triangles can be baked ahead of time and refrigerated in a single layer, covered, until ready to serve. Allow them to reach room temperature before reheating. They can also be frozen in a tightly covered container—take care to stack them carefully. Reheat them, unthawed, in a 375-degree-F oven for about 15 minutes.

Almond Skordalia

MAKES ABOUT 1½ CUPS
DRYING TIME (BREAD ONLY): 24 HOURS
COOKING TIME: 10 MINUTES
PREPARATION TIME: ABOUT 25 MINUTES
CHILLING TIME: AT LEAST 4 HOURS

Nutty yet light and refreshing, this unusual almond dip is a real treat.

6 ounces (about 6 slices) firm home-style white bread
1 small all-purpose potato (about 3 ounces), peeled and quartered
1/2 cup coarsely chopped blanched almonds
5 large cloves garlic, minced
3 tablespoons extra-virgin olive oil
2 tablespoons white wine vinegar
1 tablespoon plus 1 teaspoon fresh lemon juice, or more to taste
1/2 teaspoon sugar
3/4 teaspoon salt, or more to taste
Pinch of freshly ground white pepper, or more to taste

1 Assemble *mise en place* trays for this recipe (see page 7).

2 Trim the crusts from the bread. If not sliced, cut into slices. Lay the slices in a single layer on a baking sheet and let air-dry for 24 hours, turning from time to time.

3 In a small saucepan, cover the potatoes with cool water and bring to a boil over medium heat. Reduce the heat and simmer for about 6 minutes, or until very soft. Remove from the heat, drain, and set aside to cool. Transfer the potatoes to a food processor fitted with the metal blade. Add the almonds and garlic and process until smooth.

4 In a small bowl, combine the oil, vinegar, lemon juice, sugar, salt, and white pepper. Set aside.

5 Fill a large bowl with cool water. One at a time, drop in the dry bread slices. When well soaked, remove and squeeze out most of the water from each slice. The bread should still be moist. With the food processor running, alternately add the bread and the oil mixture to the almond mixture, and process until very smooth. Taste and adjust the seasonings with additional lemon juice, salt, and/or pepper. Transfer to a nonreactive container, cover, and refrigerate for about 4 hours, or until well chilled. If the mixture seems too stiff, beat in a little water. Serve chilled, with pita chips if desired.

White Beans with Garlic

MAKES ABOUT 4½ CUPS
SOAKING TIME (BEANS ONLY): 12 HOURS
COOKING TIME: ABOUT 1 HOUR AND 40 MINUTES
PREPARATION TIME: ABOUT 10 MINUTES
CHILLING TIME: AT LEAST 4 HOURS

These huge lima beans have a buttery flavor and creamy texture, which make a fabulous amalgam on the appetizer table. For a perfect match, serve with Skordalia.

1 pound dried gigandes (giant white lima beans)
1½ teaspoons salt
1/2 cup extra-virgin olive oil
1/4 teaspoon freshly ground white pepper
1 tablespoon chopped fresh flat-leaf parsley
6 to 8 sprigs fresh flat-leaf parsley

1 Assemble *mise en place* trays for this recipe (see page 7).

2 Check through the beans and remove any damaged ones or foreign matter. Place in a large bowl and add enough cold water to cover. Discard any beans or skins that float to the surface. Drain in a colander, rinse under cold running water, and return the beans to the bowl. Cover with cold water and soak for 12 hours, or overnight.

3 Drain the beans and transfer to a large heavy saucepan. Add enough cold water to cover by about 1 inch and bring to a boil over high heat. Boil for about 10 minutes, skimming off any foam as it rises to the surface. Add 1 teaspoon salt, reduce the heat, cover, and simmer, stirring occasionally, for 1½ hours, or until the beans are fork-tender. Drain, transfer to a bowl, and cool for about 15 minutes, or until the beans stop steaming but are still very warm.

4 In a small bowl, whisk together the oil, the remaining 1/2 teaspoon salt, the white pepper, and chopped parsley. Pour over the warm beans and toss gently to coat. Cover and refrigerate for at least 4 hours, or until well chilled and the flavors have blended. Serve at room temperature, garnished with the parsley sprigs.

Fillet of Snapper with Tomato, Onion, and Garlic

This traditional fish preparation is found in homes and restaurants throughout Greece. Its popularity is equaled only by its aromatic flavor and ease of preparation.

1/3 cup plus 2 tablespoons olive oil
1 1/2 cups chopped onions
1 cup thinly sliced carrots
3 cloves garlic, sliced
1 1/4 cups dry white wine
Two 14 1/2-ounce cans whole tomatoes, drained and chopped
1 cup water
1/4 cup plus 2 tablespoons chopped fresh flat-leaf parsley
Salt and freshly ground black pepper to taste
Six 6-ounce fillets red snapper, skin on

1 Assemble *mise en place* trays for this recipe (see page 7).

2 In a large heavy skillet, heat 1/3 cup of the oil over medium heat. Add the onions, carrots, and garlic and sauté for about 10 minutes, or until very soft but not browned. Stir in the wine and cook, stirring occasionally, for about 15 minutes, or until the wine has evaporated. Stir in the tomatoes, water, 1/4 cup of the parsley, and salt and pepper to taste, and bring to a boil. Reduce the heat and simmer, uncovered, for about 15 minutes, stirring frequently, until slightly thickened. Set aside to cool slightly.

3 Preheat the oven to 400 degrees F.

4 Rub both sides of the fish with the remaining 2 tablespoons olive oil. Season lightly with salt and pepper and set aside.

5 Spoon about a third of the tomato sauce into a shallow baking dish just large enough to hold the fillets. Arrange the fish, skin side down, on the sauce. Spoon the remaining sauce over the fish and bake for about 12 minutes, or until the fish flakes easily when tested with a fork and the sauce is bubbling.

6 Place the fillets on warm plates, spoon the sauce over, and sprinkle with the remaining 2 tablespoons parsley. Serve immediately, with rice or couscous if desired.

NOTE: You can replace the red snapper with striped bass, black sea bass, or any other firm-fleshed, nonfatty fish fillets.

■ An easy method for chopping canned tomatoes is to cut them up in the can using clean kitchen shears.

CHARLES BOWMAN: *Fillet of Snapper with Tomato, Onion, and Garlic*

Baklava

Known throughout the world as *the* Greek dessert, flaky baklava is incredibly sweet—and incredibly delicious.

2 cups toasted walnuts

2 cups blanched almonds

16 pieces zweibach (or 1 cup dry bread crumbs)

1 tablespoon ground cinnamon

2 tablespoons unsalted butter, softened

One 1-pound package phyllo dough, thawed according to the package directions

1 1/2 cups Clarified Butter (see page 9), melted

About 18 whole cloves

3 cups sugar

2 1/4 cups water

3/4 cup honey

One 3-inch cinnamon stick

2 tablespoons brandy

■ Special Equipment: Pizza cutter (optional)

1 Assemble *mise en place* trays for this recipe (see page 7).

2 Place half of the walnuts and almonds in a food processor fitted with the metal blade. Chop fine, using quick pulses and being careful not to pulverize. Transfer to a large bowl. Repeat with the remaining nuts and add to the bowl.

3 Place half of the zweibach in the food processor and process to make fine crumbs. Add to the nuts. Repeat with the remaining zweibach. Add the cinnamon to the nut-crumb mixture and toss to blend.

4 Preheat the oven to 350 degrees F. Butter a 13 x 9-inch glass baking dish with the softened butter.

5 Lay the phyllo sheets on a dry work surface. With a pizza cutter or a long sharp knife, cut the phyllo crosswise in half to make 2 stacks of 12 x 8 1/2-inch sheets. Lay 4 sheets in the pan. (Since the phyllo is not quite long enough to cover the bottom of the pan completely, as you assemble the baklava, alternate the sheets so that every other layer, more or less, reaches the opposite ends of the pan.) Using a pastry brush, coat the sheets of phyllo with clarified butter. Repeat to make 8 layers of phyllo, leaving the final sheet dry.

6 Sprinkle about 1 1/4 cups of the nut mixture over the dry sheet of phyllo. Add 4 more sheets of phyllo, brushing each one with butter but leaving the final sheet dry. Sprinkle with another 1 1/4 cups of the nut mixture. Repeat this procedure two more times, ending with a layer of nuts. Add the remaining sheets of phyllo, brushing each one including the top one with butter.

7 With a long sharp knife, cut the baklava lengthwise into thirds. Then cut these strips on the diagonal into diamond shapes, ending just short of the lengthwise cuts and the sides of the pan. With a short spatula, work around the sides of the pan, tucking the layers of dough in so that the edges are smooth. Stick a clove into the center of each diamond. Bake for about 1 hour, or until golden brown on top. Set on a wire rack to cool completely.

8 In a large saucepan, combine the sugar, water, honey, cinnamon stick, and 3 cloves and bring to a boil over medium heat, stirring with a wooden spoon until the sugar dissolves. Reduce the heat slightly and boil gently for about 10 minutes, until slightly syrupy. Remove from the heat and stir in the brandy. Set aside to cool to lukewarm.

9 Pour the syrup over the cooled baklava. Cover loosely and set aside at room temperature for several hours, or overnight. Finish cutting the baklava just before serving.

CHARLES BOWMAN: *Baklava*

23

FLAVORS OF THE SUN

Toasted Couscous Risotto

Roast Poussin with Green Olives,
Preserved Lemon, and Garlic

Quick Preserved Lemons

Lemon Curd Napoleon

WINE SUGGESTIONS:

Sauvignon Blanc or Pinot Grigio *(first course)*

Beaujolais or Barbera d'Asti *(second course)*

Late-Harvest Riesling (German or California) *(dessert)*

WHAT YOU CAN PREPARE AHEAD OF TIME

Up to 1 week ahead: Make the Preserved Lemons. Prepare the Chicken Stock (if making your own). Make the Clarified Butter.

Up to 3 days ahead: Make the lemon curd for the Lemon Curd Napoleon.

Up to 2 days ahead: Marinate the chicken for the Roast Poussin.

Early in the day: Prepare the ingredients for the Toasted Couscous Risotto. Roast the garlic for the Roast Poussin, cover, and set aside at room temperature. Bake the phyllo discs, cover, and set aside at room temperature. Clean the raspberries, cover, and refrigerate.

I first met Terrance Brennan in, of all places, the Dominican Republic. He had just finished a stint apprenticing with many of the three-star chefs of France and had taken a break to assist my husband, Alain Sailhac, at the restaurants in Casa de Campo. These jobs, plus his work in many celebrated New York restaurants, were the preparation he needed to achieve his dream: a restaurant of his own. In his travels, the flavors of the Mediterranean had won his heart and so when he was able to, he opened one of the first Mediterranean restaurants in Manhattan. Called Picholine, after the succulent green olive that grows in the South of France, the warm, comfortable bistro has brought a taste of the sun to the city canyons. Terry's menu clearly demonstrates how he has expanded on classical recipes and made them his own. He is truly one of America's great young chefs.

◁ TERRANCE BRENNAN: *Lemon Curd Napoleon*

Toasted Couscous Risotto

This is an absolutely delicious play on classic Italian risotto. And it requires much less stirring time at the stove.

2¹/₂ cups Chicken Stock (see page 10)
¹/₂ cup dry white wine
2 tablespoons olive oil
¹/₂ cup chopped onions
1 tablespoon minced garlic
Pinch of salt, plus more to taste
2 cups toasted Israeli couscous
5 ounces fresh morels, cooked (about 1¹/₂ cups cooked; see Note)
18 medium-sized spears asparagus, trimmed, cut into 1-inch lengths, and blanched
18 ramps or baby leeks, trimmed and blanched
1 cup shelled fresh fava beans or peas, blanched
¹/₂ cup freshly grated Parmesan cheese
3 tablespoons white truffle oil
3 tablespoons unsalted butter, at room temperature
¹/₄ cup chopped fresh flat-leaf parsley
¹/₄ cup snipped fresh chives
Freshly ground white pepper to taste
Parmesan cheese, for shaving

1 Assemble *mise en place* trays for this recipe (see page 7).

2 In a bowl or large glass measuring cup, combine the stock and wine. Set aside.

3 In a medium-sized saucepan, heat the oil over medium heat. Add the onions, garlic, and a pinch of salt and cook for about 4 minutes, or until just softened. Add the couscous and 2 cups of the stock mixture and cook, stirring occasionally, for about 15 minutes, or until all the liquid has been absorbed. Add the remaining stock mixture and cook for about 4 minutes, beating rapidly with a wooden spoon until the couscous softens and plumps. Stir in the morels, asparagus, ramps, and fava beans and cook for 1 minute.

4 Remove the pan from the heat and stir in the grated cheese, truffle oil, butter, parsley, and chives. Season to taste with salt and white pepper.

5 Spoon into warm shallow soup bowls and garnish with shavings of Parmesan. Serve immediately.

NOTE: Cook the morels by sautéing them in a small amount of olive oil or butter until just tender. If you can't find morels, use any type of small, earthy mushrooms of equal size or use common button mushrooms.

■ Large-grained Israeli couscous does not require the constant stirring rice does when making traditional risotto; stir it only enough to keep it from sticking.

TERRANCE BRENNAN: *Toasted Couscous Risotto*

Roast Poussin with Green Olives, Preserved Lemon, and Garlic

SERVES 6
MARINATING TIME: 48 HOURS
PREPARATION TIME: ABOUT 25 MINUTES
COOKING TIME: ABOUT 20 MINUTES

This perfect marriage of flavors is a real crowd pleaser. The saffron provides a rather haunting flavor of exotic places and the preserved lemons add a refreshing zing.

6 poussin, backbones removed
1½ cups olive oil
1 tablespoon chopped garlic
1 tablespoon grated lemon zest
3 pinches of powdered saffron
40 roasted garlic cloves (see page 9), 10 peeled and 30 left unpeeled
1¼ cups Chicken Stock (see page 10)
2 tablespoons Dijon mustard
1½ cups pitted Picholine olives
Preserved Lemons (recipe follows), well drained
¼ cup chopped fresh cilantro
Salt and freshly ground black pepper to taste

■ Special Equipment: Hand-held immersion blender (optional)

1 Assemble *mise en place* trays for this recipe (see page 7).

2 Place the poussin in a glass baking dish large enough to hold them comfortably when laid out flat and add ½ cup of the olive oil, the chopped garlic, lemon zest, and saffron. Toss to coat, cover, and refrigerate for 2 days, turning occasionally.

3 Preheat the oven to 500 degrees F.

4 Drain the excess oil from the poussin and place in a roasting pan, skin side up. Bake for about 20 minutes, or until the poussin are just cooked and the skin is crisp.

5 Meanwhile, in a medium-sized saucepan, bring the stock to a boil over medium heat. Remove the pan from the heat, add the peeled garlic cloves and mustard, and blend well with a hand-held immersion blender or a whisk, until the garlic is pureed. Slowly blend in the remaining 1 cup oil. Stir in the olives, Preserved Lemons, and cilantro. Season with salt and pepper to taste.

6 Place a poussin on each warm plate. Spoon the sauce around the poussin and garnish each with 5 unpeeled roasted garlic cloves. Top with some of the preserved lemon zest. (Do not spoon the sauce over the poussin, or the crisp skin will get soggy.) Serve immediately.

NOTE: The poussin, very small young chickens usually weighing about 1 pound, can be replaced with 3 very small broilers, split in half.

■ A hand-held immersion blender quickly and smoothly incorporates hot ingredients into a sauce.

QUICK PRESERVED LEMONS

MAKES ABOUT 2 TABLESPOONS
PREPARATION TIME: ABOUT 5 MINUTES
COOKING TIME: ABOUT 10 MINUTES

This speedy method of preserving lemon zest makes a traditional Middle Eastern flavor accessible to the busy home cook. Once tried, you'll find a million uses for this savory taste.

Zest of 2 large blemish-free lemons, removed with a vegetable peeler or sharp knife and cut into fine julienne
3¼ cups water
2 tablespoons sugar
1 teaspoon salt

1 Assemble *mise en place* trays for this recipe (see page 7).

2 Put the lemon zest in a small nonreactive saucepan with 1 cup of cold water. Bring to a simmer over high heat and immediately remove from the heat. Drain and repeat. Drain and set aside.

3 Add the water, sugar, and salt to the saucepan and bring to a boil over high heat. Reduce the heat and simmer for about 2 minutes. Add the zest and simmer for about 5 minutes, until softened. Remove the pan from the heat and cool. Use right away or store in the cooking liquid, covered and refrigerated, for up to 2 weeks.

Lemon Curd Napoleon

SERVES 6
PREPARATION TIME: ABOUT 45 MINUTES
COOKING TIME: 4 MINUTES
BAKING TIME: ABOUT 5 MINUTES

This very sophisticated dessert combines two traditional ingredients in a most unusual way. And, as impressive as it is, it's quite easy to put together.

8 large egg yolks
1/2 cup fresh lemon juice
Grated zest of 2 lemons
3/4 cup sugar
8 tablespoons (1 stick) unsalted butter, cubed, at room temperature
6 sheets phyllo dough, thawed according to the package directions
1/2 cup Clarified Butter (see page 9), melted
1/2 cup confectioners' sugar
1 pint raspberries, washed and dried

1 Assemble *mise en place* trays for this recipe (see page 7).

2 In a medium-sized heat-proof bowl, combine the egg yolks, lemon juice, and zest. Whisk in the sugar and set the bowl over (not in) a pot of simmering water. Do not let the bottom of the bowl touch the water. Cook, whisking constantly, for about 4 minutes, or until thickened.

3 Remove the bowl from the heat and beat in the room-temperature butter, a piece at a time, until completely incorporated.

4 Put the bowl in an ice water bath and stir the curd frequently until cool. Cover and refrigerate until ready to use.

5 Preheat the oven to 400 degrees F. Line 2 baking sheets with parchment paper.

6 Place 1 phyllo sheet on a dry work surface. Using a pastry brush, liberally coat with clarified butter. Top with 2 more sheets, brushing each with butter. Make a second stack with the 3 remaining sheets of phyllo, buttering each one. Using a sharp round 3-inch cookie cutter, cut out 12 circles from each stack. Sprinkle with confectioners' sugar and arrange on the baking sheets. Cover each baking sheet with a sheet of parchment paper and put another baking sheet on top to hold the phyllo discs flat. Bake for about 5 minutes, or until golden. Remove the baking sheets and parchment from the top of the phyllo disks and cool on the baking sheets.

7 Place a small dollop of lemon curd in the center of each plate. Place a phyllo disc on top and dab each with a tablespoon of curd. Arrange 4 raspberries on the curd and top each dessert with another phyllo disc. Repeat to make 4 layers, ending with a phyllo disc. Sprinkle with confectioners' sugar and serve immediately.

NOTE: The raspberries can be replaced with any other berry except strawberries, which are too large for an attractive presentation.

◾ When washing raspberries, mist them with a sprayer and turn them upside down on paper towels to dry. If they are handled too much, they tend to disintegrate.

◾ The curd can be made with any citrus fruit.

◁ TERRANCE BRENNAN: *Roast Poussin with Green Olives, Preserved Lemon, and Garlic*

GREAT SUNNY FLAVORS

Seared Scallops in Gazpacho-Thyme Sauce

Vegetable Paella

Coffee Granita with Lemon-Scented Ice Milk

BLANCO Y NEGRO

WINE SUGGESTIONS:

Sauvignon Blanc *(first course)*

Sparkling Wine or Beer *(second course)*

WHAT YOU CAN PREPARE AHEAD OF TIME

Up to 1 week ahead: Prepare the Vegetable Stock (if making your own).

Up to 2 days ahead: Prepare the milk mixture for the Lemon-Scented Ice Milk.

Up to 1 day ahead: Make the Gazpacho Thyme Sauce. Make the Coffee Granita and Lemon-Scented Ice Milk.

Early in the day: Julienne, salt, and drain the vegetables for the Vegetable Paella, cover, and refrigerate. Blanch the vegetables for the paella, cover, and refrigerate.

Dominick Cerrone first made his mark at the famed Le Bernardin in New York City. His Spanish roots and childhood memories served him well as a most talented master of fine fish dishes with origins in Spain. However, when he wanted to recreate the tastes of his family table more clearly, he opened Solera, a modern Spanish bistro, in Manhattan. Here, he updated his memories with the techniques and flavors he had learned as a professional chef to bring a worldly menu to sophisticated diners. In the recipes he shared with us at De Gustibus, we were given a sunny taste of the Mediterranean in a new and exciting way.

◁ DOMINICK CERRONE: *Vegetable Paella*

Seared Scallops in Gazpacho-Thyme Sauce

SERVES 6
PREPARATION TIME: ABOUT 1 HOUR
COOKING TIME: ABOUT 7 MINUTES

The ubiquitous gazpacho reaches a totally new dimension when it's served as a sauce for sea scallops. The zesty flavors intermingle with the sweet, firm-fleshed shellfish, giving new meaning to the opening of a fine meal.

SAUCE:

1 red bell pepper, cored, seeded, and chopped
1/2 green bell pepper, cored, seeded, and chopped
1/2 yellow bell pepper, cored, seeded, and chopped
1 large ripe tomato, cored and chopped
1 rib celery, chopped
1/2 hothouse cucumber, chopped
1/4 small onion, chopped
1 clove garlic, chopped
6 fresh basil leaves, chopped
2 cups plus 1 tablespoon tomato juice
2 tablespoons plus 1 teaspoon sherry wine vinegar
1 tablespoon extra-virgin olive oil
Fine sea salt and freshly ground white pepper to taste
Pinch of cayenne pepper, or to taste
1 large sprig fresh thyme

SCALLOPS:

1/2 hothouse cucumber, cut into fine julienne (avoid the seedy center)
1 small zucchini, trimmed and cut into fine julienne (avoid the seedy center)
1 small yellow squash, trimmed and cut into fine julienne (avoid the seedy center)
Fine sea salt to taste
1 red bell pepper, cored, seeded, and finely diced
1/2 green bell pepper, cored, seeded, and finely diced
1/2 yellow bell pepper, cored, seeded, and finely diced
30 sea scallops
Freshly ground white pepper to taste
2 tablespoons extra-virgin olive oil
1 tablespoon fresh thyme leaves
6 small sprigs fresh thyme

1 Assemble *mise en place* trays for this recipe (see page 7).

2 To make the sauce, in a food processor fitted with the metal blade, combine the chopped bell peppers, tomatoes, celery, cucumbers, onions, garlic, basil, tomato juice, vinegar, and oil. Process until smooth. (For a more refined sauce, strain through a fine sieve.) Transfer to a nonreactive container and season to taste with salt and white pepper and cayenne. Add the thyme sprig and set aside.

3 To prepare the scallops, in a colander, combine the cucumber, zucchini, and yellow squash. Lightly salt and toss well. Set the colander on a plate and drain for about 15

DOMINICK CERRONE: *Seared Scallops in Gazpacho-Thyme Sauce*

minutes. Rinse the vegetables under cold running water, pat dry, and lay on paper towels.

4 In a large saucepan of boiling water, blanch the bell peppers for 10 seconds. Drain, rinse under cold running water, and pat dry. Set aside.

5 Wash the scallops and pat dry with paper towels. Season to taste with salt and white pepper. In a large nonstick skillet, heat the oil over high heat. Add the scallops and sear for about 3 minutes, or until golden on the bottom. Turn and sear for 2 minutes longer, or until the scallops are golden on both sides and firm to the touch. Transfer to a warm baking sheet and cover to keep warm.

6 In the same skillet, sauté the julienned vegetables for 1 minute, or just until they absorb some scallop flavor and soften slightly. Do not overcook.

7 Pour about ¼ cup of the sauce onto the center of each plate and allow to spread to cover the plate. Sprinkle the diced peppers over the sauce. Pile equal portions of julienned vegetables in the center of each plate and surround with an equal number of scallops (or create a balanced design of your choice with the julienned vegetables and scallops). Sprinkle with the fresh thyme leaves and garnish each plate with a thyme sprig. Serve immediately.

NOTE: The julienned vegetables are salted and drained to reduce their moisture content so that they do not release liquid into the sauté pan.

■ Chef Cerrone suggests canned Sacramento-brand tomato juice and either a spicy green Lerida olive oil or a sweet yellow oil from southern Spain.

■ You will have lots of extra sauce, which you can use to garnish other fish dishes or chicken or as a salad or vegetable dressing. The sauce may also be frozen for up to 1 month.

Vegetable Paella

SERVES 6
PREPARATION TIME: ABOUT 1½ HOURS
COOKING TIME: ABOUT 30 MINUTES

This is a dazzling vegetarian dish that can be adapted to any time of the year using fresh seasonal vegetables. When presented at the table, it resembles an edible kaleidoscope.

1 large tomato, peeled, cored, seeded, and chopped
2 tablespoons minced onion
7 cups Vegetable Stock (see page 11)
1½ tablespoons saffron threads
1½ tablespoons Hungarian paprika
1 bay leaf
⅓ cup extra-virgin olive oil
3 cups Arborio rice
½ cup fresh peas
⅓ cup diced roasted red bell pepper
½ to ¾ cup each of at least 6 of the following: blanched sliced carrots, fennel, celery, asparagus, and/or artichoke hearts; blanched corn kernels, sliced broccoli, and/or sliced cauliflower florets; blanched trimmed string beans, sugar snap peas, snow peas, and/or sliced mushrooms; shredded spinach and/or endive

¼ cup chopped fresh herbs [1 tablespoon each parsley and chives combined with any other herb(s) you desire]
Olive oil spray (optional)

■ **Special Equipment:** Paella pan or other wide shallow two-handled pan (about 14 inches in diameter)

1 Assemble *mise en place* trays for this recipe (see page 7).

2 In a small bowl, toss the tomatoes and onions to combine.

3 In a medium-sized saucepan, combine the stock, saffron, paprika, bay leaf, and tomato mixture and bring to a boil over medium-high heat. Immediately reduce the heat to a simmer.

4 Heat the paella pan over medium-high heat. Add the oil and when very hot, stir in the rice. Cook, stirring constantly, for about 3 minutes, or until golden brown. Add 6 cups of the simmering stock, reduce the heat until barely simmering, and cook, without stirring, for about 20 minutes, or until the rice is barely *al dente* (see Note); place the vegetables decoratively over the rice as it cooks. Begin with the peas and roasted peppers and add the other vegetables according to the degree of doneness you desire. When the rice is *al dente,* turn off the heat and rest for about 10 minutes.

5 Sprinkle the paella with the herbs and, if desired, spray a

bit of olive oil spray over the dish to make it glisten. Serve immediately, bringing the pan to the table.

NOTE: The extra cup of stock should be added if all the liquid has been absorbed before the rice is done. When setting up the decorative vegetable pattern, use one vegetable, such as asparagus, to outline sections.

■ If the paella pan is larger than the stove burner, set it off center and rotate it frequently for even cooking.

Coffee Granita with Lemon-Scented Ice Milk

SERVES 6
INFUSING TIME (MILK MIXTURE ONLY): 12 HOURS
PREPARATION TIME: ABOUT 30 MINUTES
FREEZING TIME: 2 HOURS

Blanco y Negro

Here is a summer dessert that is perfection! Because it is icy-cold, it must be made well in advance. The granita is wonderfully invigorating, rather like eating a refreshing frozen cappuccino.

2/3 cup plus 6 tablespoons granulated sugar
3 cups milk
1 cup heavy cream
Zest of 1 large lemon, removed with a vegetable peeler or sharp knife and cut into strips
One 3-inch cinnamon stick
3 cups very hot espresso (or other strong coffee)
4 large egg whites, at room temperature
Cocoa for dusting (optional)
6 sprigs fresh mint
■ Special Equipment: Hand-held immersion blender

1 Assemble *mise en place* trays for this recipe (see page 7).

2 In a medium-sized saucepan, combine the 2/3 cup sugar with the milk, cream, lemon zest, and cinnamon stick and bring to a boil over medium heat, stirring to dissolve the sugar. Immediately remove the pan from the heat and pour into a nonreactive container. Cover and refrigerate for at least 12 hours.

3 Dissolve 3 tablespoons of the remaining sugar in the coffee and pour onto a rimmed baking sheet. Place in the

freezer and freeze, frequently breaking up the frozen edges with a fork to prevent the mixture from freezing in a solid block. When completely frozen, transfer to a small freezer container and keep frozen.

4 Put a 9 x 13-inch pan in the freezer. Place 6 goblets or coupes in the refrigerator.

5 In a large bowl, using an electric mixer set at medium-high speed, beat the egg whites with the remaining 3 tablespoons sugar until they hold stiff peaks. Refrigerate this meringue.

6 Using a hand-held immersion blender, whip the chilled milk mixture until it holds firm peaks. Fold into the chilled meringue, scrape into the chilled pan, cover, and freeze for 2 hours.

7 When ready to serve, scrape the coffee granita *(Negro)* into the chilled goblets. Place a scoop of ice milk *(Blanco)* on top. Serve immediately, dusted with cocoa if desired, garnishing each with a mint sprig and a cookie.

NOTE: You could also flavor the ice milk with either lemon grass or lemon verbena.

DOMINICK CERRONE: *Coffee Granita with Lemon-Scented Ice Milk* ▷

A MAGICAL MEDITERRANEAN BUFFET

Baba Ganoush

Sofrito of Baby Lamb with Romesco Sauce

Fattoush

Blueberry Clafoutis

WINE SUGGESTIONS:

Champagne *(first course)*

Merlot or Pinot Noir *(second course—lamb and fattoush)*

Ruby Port *(dessert)*

WHAT YOU CAN PREPARE AHEAD OF TIME

Up to 2 days ahead: Prepare the Baba Ganoush and the Romesco Sauce.

Up to 1 day ahead: Chop the vegetables for the Sofrito of Baby Lamb. Place in a plastic bag and refrigerate. Bake the pita for the Fattoush. Make the dressing for the Fattoush, cover, and refrigerate.

Early in the day: Prepare the Sofrito of Baby Lamb. Reheat for about 15 minutes in a 325-degree-F oven before serving. Prepare the vegetables and herbs for the Fattoush. Place in plastic bags and refrigerate. Make the Blueberry Clafoutis. Reheat for about 10 minutes in a 300-degree-F oven before serving.

Andy D'Amico is a De Gustibus treasure. Over the years, he has taught many classes, always pleasantly surprising us with the versatility of his repertoire. Executive Chef at New York's Sign of the Dove and partner with Joe, Berge, and Henny Santo in a host of other restaurants, Andy presented this buffet as a home cook's dream. I had enjoyed a similar table at The Sign of the Dove at a baby shower given for a dear friend, Dorothy Cann Hamilton, the founder of The French Culinary Institute in New York City. At both the party and the De Gustibus class, all the dishes stood up to the demands of an evening sitting out on the table. They were all prepared in advance and offered an abundance of flavors that married well.

◁ ANDREW D'AMICO: *Baba Ganoush, Sofrito of Lamb with Romesco Sauce, Fattoush, and Blueberry Clafoutis*

Baba Ganoush

Andy's tangy version of the famous Lebanese dip has the added flavor of smoky eggplant. For a stunning visual effect, complete the dish with the traditional pomegranate seed garnish. Serve this with pita bread, crackers, or toasted country-style bread rubbed with garlic.

1 large eggplant, about 1 pound
2 cloves garlic
1/4 to 1/3 cup fresh lemon juice
Salt to taste
2 to 4 tablespoons tahini
2 tablespoons olive oil
Ground cumin to taste
Freshly ground black pepper to taste

GARNISH (OPTIONAL)

3 tablespoons pomegranate seeds, or 1 tablespoon chopped fresh flat-leaf parsley, or 1/8 teaspoon ground sumac, or 1 tablespoon extra-virgin olive oil

1 Assemble *mise en place* trays for this recipe (see page 7).

2 Prepare a charcoal or gas grill or preheat the broiler.

3 Using a fork, puncture the eggplant in several places. Roast the eggplant on the grill or under the broiler for about 20 minutes, turning occasionally, until the skin is completely charred and the eggplant is soft. Cool until cool enough to handle. Halve and scrape out the pulp, put it in a fine sieve, and hold under gently running cold water to wash away any bitterness. Shake dry and use your hands to squeeze out as much liquid as possible.

4 In a food processor fitted with the metal blade, combine the eggplant pulp, garlic, 1/4 cup lemon juice, and salt to taste. Process until smooth. Add 2 tablespoons tahini and process just to incorporate. Taste and, if necessary, adjust the flavors with additional lemon juice and tahini. With the processor running, add the oil. Season to taste with cumin, salt, and pepper. Transfer to a small serving bowl, cover, and chill for at least 30 minutes, or up to 2 days.

5 Garnish with pomegranate seeds, parsley, sumac, or a drizzle of olive oil if desired, and serve.

NOTE: To retrieve pomegranate seeds neatly, barely cut into the tough skin and then peel it back as you would peel an orange. The seeds will fall out without staining your hands with the intense red juice.

ANDREW D'AMICO: *Baba Ganoush*

Sofrito of Baby Lamb with Romesco Sauce

This succulent dish traces its beginnings to the Spanish countryside. This is served with the meat removed from the bone and kept warm in a beautiful chafing dish. If serving the lamb as an entrée, add roasted potatoes and a crisp green vegetable.

1/4 **cup olive oil**
One 6-pound leg of lamb
2 bulbs garlic, split in half crosswise
2 cups finely diced onions
1 cup finely diced fennel
2 sprigs fresh thyme
2 sprigs fresh rosemary
2 sprigs fresh cilantro
2 bay leaves
Romesco Sauce (recipe follows)
Coarse salt to taste

1 Assemble *mise en place* trays for this recipe (see page 7).

2 Preheat the oven to 350 degrees F.

3 In a roasting pan or casserole with a tight-fitting lid, heat the oil over medium heat. Add the lamb and sear, turning frequently, for about 6 minutes, or until brown on all sides.

4 Add the garlic, onions, and fennel and sauté for about 10 minutes, or until the vegetables are golden brown. Add the thyme, rosemary, cilantro, bay leaves, and 3 cups of water. Cover and roast for 45 minutes.

5 Turn the meat and check the water level. If the vegetables look dry, add 1 more cup of water. Continue to roast, turning and adding water, 1/2 cup at a time, when necessary, for an additional 1 hour and 15 minutes.

6 Using a pastry brush, thinly coat the lamb on all sides with Romesco Sauce. Sprinkle with salt. Cover and return to the oven for 1 hour longer.

7 Turn the lamb, brush with Romesco Sauce, and season with coarse salt. Return to the oven, uncovered, and roast for approximately 45 minutes longer, or until the meat easily falls from the bone. Transfer to a large chafing dish and serve with the remaining sauce on the side.

ANDREW D'AMICO: *Sofrito of Lamb with Romesco Sauce*

ROMESCO SAUCE
MAKES ABOUT 1 1/2 CUPS

3 plum tomatoes, halved
2 fresh hot green chiles, such as jalapeño or serrano, halved and seeded
1 red bell pepper, cored, quartered, and seeded
1 small bulb garlic, separated into cloves
1/2 **cup sliced unblanched almonds**
1 dried New Mexican red chile
1 cup water
3 tablespoons red wine vinegar
2 tablespoons chopped fresh flat-leaf parsley
1 tablespoon sweet paprika
1/2 **cup olive oil**
Salt and freshly ground black pepper to taste

1 Preheat the oven to 350 degrees F.

2 Place the tomatoes, fresh chiles, bell pepper, garlic, and almonds on a nonstick baking sheet, keeping each ingredient separate, and bake for about 20 minutes, removing the items as they are cooked: The almonds will brown quickly, while the vegetables will probably require the full time for their skins to blister and their flesh to soften. Cool, then peel the peppers and garlic. Finely chop the almonds in a spice grinder or finely grind them with a mortar and pestle.

3 In a small saucepan, combine the dried chile and water and bring to a boil over high heat. Reduce the heat and simmer for about 10 minutes, or until the liquid is reduced to 1/4 cup. Remove the pan from the heat and cool slightly. Seed and stem the chile and set aside. Reserve the cooking water.

4 In a food processor fitted with the metal blade, combine the green chiles, bell pepper, garlic, dried chile and cooking water, vinegar, parsley, and paprika and process until smooth. With the processor running, slowly add the oil. When well blended, season to taste with salt and pepper. Transfer to a nonreactive bowl and fold in the almonds. Use immediately or cover and refrigerate until ready to use.

■ Any leftover sauce can be used as a base for a soup or as a glaze for grilled meats.

■ You can cook veal shanks, beef shanks, or rack of lamb or rack of veal in this manner. The sauce also serves as a glaze for roast rack of lamb.

Fattoush

SERVES 6
PREPARATION TIME: ABOUT 30 MINUTES
TOASTING TIME: ABOUT 10 MINUTES

This hearty bread salad has its roots in Syria. Related to the Tuscan panzanella, an equally filling side dish, fattoush is an excellent accompaniment to grilled or roasted meats.

6 day-old 6-inch pita breads, cut into 1/2-inch squares
2 cloves garlic, minced
1 serrano chile, seeded and minced
1 teaspoon salt, plus more to taste
1/2 cup fresh lemon juice
1/2 teaspoon ground sumac
1/4 cup extra-virgin olive oil
1/4 cup virgin olive oil
Freshly ground black pepper to taste
3 large ripe but firm tomatoes, peeled, cored, seeded, and cut into 1/4-inch dice
2 scallions, cut into 1/4-inch dice
1 small red onion, cut into 1/4-inch dice
1 small red bell pepper, cored, seeded, and cut into 1/4-inch dice
1 large cucumber, peeled, seeded, and cut into 1/4-inch dice
1 large head Romaine lettuce, inner leaves only, coarsely chopped
1/2 cup chopped fresh flat-leaf parsley
1/2 cup chopped fresh mint
1/2 cup chopped fresh cilantro

■ Special Equipment: Mini food processor

1 Assemble *mise en place* trays for this recipe (see page 7).

2 Preheat the oven to 350 degrees F.

3 Place the pita on a nonstick baking sheet and bake for 10 minutes, or until golden brown. Set aside.

ANDREW D'AMICO: *Fattoush*

4 In a mini food processor fitted with the metal blade (or in a mortar and pestle), process (or grind) the garlic, chile, and salt until a paste forms. Transfer to a small bowl and stir in the lemon juice and sumac. Whisk in the oils and season to taste with salt, if necessary, and pepper.

5 In a salad bowl, combine the tomatoes, scallions, onions, bell peppers, cucumbers, lettuce, parsley, mint, and cilantro. Add the dressing and toss to combine. Toss in the toasted pita and serve immediately.

Blueberry Clafoutis

SERVES 6 TO 8
PREPARATION TIME: ABOUT 20 MINUTES
BAKING TIME: ABOUT 40 MINUTES

This easy-to-prepare, pudding-like dessert is always well received, especially if the fruit is ripe and sweet. Although French, clafoutis is not from the Mediterranean area but from the Limousin region, where it is traditionally made with dark, juicy cherries.

1/2 cup plus 2 tablespoons confectioners' sugar
2 large egg yolks
1 large egg
8 tablespoons (1 stick) unsalted butter, cut into pieces, softened
1 cup all-purpose flour
1 cup hot boiled milk
2 tablespoons kirschwasser, rum, or Chambord
2 1/2 cups ripe blueberries, picked over, rinsed, and dried

■ **Special Equipment: 9-inch round flan dish or cake pan**

1 Assemble *mise en place* trays for this recipe (see page 7).

2 Preheat the oven to 400 degrees F. Generously butter a 9-inch flan dish or cake pan.

3 In a large bowl, using an electric mixer set on medium speed, beat 1/2 cup of the sugar and the egg yolks for 2 to 3 minutes, or until thick. Beat in the whole egg and then gradually beat in the butter, a piece at a time. Beat in the flour. Beat in the milk and kirschwasser and mix until smooth.

4 Pour into the prepared pan and distribute the berries evenly over the top. Bake on the lower rack of the oven for about 40 minutes, or until the top is golden and the center is set. Cool on a wire rack for 10 minutes. Sprinkle with the remaining 2 tablespoons sugar and serve warm.

NOTE: Any ripe berry can be used in place of or in combination with the blueberries. If the berries are not naturally sweet, toss with 1/4 cup of sugar and let stand for 30 minutes before adding to the batter. The clafoutis will be puffed when it comes out of the oven, similar to a soufflé, and although it deflates quickly, it will still taste delicious.

ANDREW D'AMICO: *Blueberry Clafoutis*

A MODERN MEDITERRANEAN DINNER PARTY

Asparagus with Red Onion Vinaigrette

Roast Salmon with Moroccan Spices

Grain Pilaf

*Gratin of Strawberries and Rhubarb with Warm Nutmeg Cream
and Pistachio Ice Cream*

WINE SUGGESTIONS:

Gavi or Dry Riesling *(first course)*

Tavel Rosé or Côtes-du-Rhône *(second course)*

WHAT YOU CAN PREPARE AHEAD OF TIME

Up to 1 week ahead: Make the Pistachio Ice Cream.

Early in the day: Prepare the asparagus, peppers, and vinaigrette for the Asparagus with Red Onion Vinaigrette. Cover and refrigerate; bring to room temperature before serving. Prepare the spice mixture for the Roast Salmon with Moroccan Spices. Cover and refrigerate. Bake the Gratin of Strawberries and Rhubarb. Reheat at 300 degrees F for 20 minutes before serving. Make the Warm Nutmeg Cream. Cover and refrigerate; reheat just before serving.

Gary Danko represented the West Coast style of Mediterranean cooking at De Gustibus. Currently Executive Chef at the Dining Room of the Ritz-Carlton Hotel in San Francisco, Gary first came to my attention at a private home on Manhattan's West Side, where he prepared a special buffet with his mentor, Madelene Kamman, the esteemed cooking teacher and writer. The meal was so colorful and so evocative of a Mediterranean summer, and the food so deceptively easy to prepare, I felt his was a style perfectly accessible for the home cook. The De Gustibus students agreed!

Although Gary has an affinity for the foods from the Mediterranean regions, his cooking is truly a personal interpretation, showcasing marriages of ingredients that distinctively blend together. His most sophisticated technique uses only a few ingredients melded to achieve maximum flavor. Gary's enthusiasm translates well to the classroom, where he is a marvelous teacher, clear in direction and succinct in preparation.

◁ GARY DANKO: *Roast Salmon with Moroccan Spices* and *Grain Pilaf*

Asparagus with Red Onion Vinaigrette

A delicious salad that could stand on its own as a main-course lunch dish, this enticing combination has its roots in Italy. Light and easy to prepare, with many components made in advance, it is a perfect addition to any entertaining menu.

2 pounds pencil-thin asparagus, trimmed to equal lengths
2 tablespoons tarragon vinegar
1 tablespoon Dijon mustard
Coarse salt and freshly ground black pepper to taste
1/4 cup plus 2 tablespoons extra-virgin olive oil
1/4 cup minced red onion
2 tablespoons drained capers
1 clove garlic, minced
2 teaspoons minced fresh tarragon
2 roasted red or yellow bell peppers, peeled, seeded, and cut lengthwise into 1/4-inch-wide strips
1/4 cup plus 2 tablespoons freshly grated Parmigiano-Reggiano cheese
12 oil-cured black olives
Parmigiano-Reggiano shavings

1 Assemble *mise en place* trays for this recipe (see page 7).

2 In a large pot of boiling water, blanch the asparagus for about 2 minutes, or until tender and bright green. Immediately drain and place in an ice water bath. When chilled, drain and pat dry.

3 In a small bowl, combine the vinegar, mustard, and coarse salt and pepper to taste. Slowly whisk in the oil until emulsified. Whisk in the onions, capers, garlic, and tarragon. Taste and adjust the seasonings. Set aside.

4 Place equal portions of asparagus on each plate, all facing in the same direction with the bases together and the stalks fanning out. Make a lattice of pepper strips covering the base of each fan. Drizzle the vinaigrette over the asparagus and sprinkle with the grated cheese. Garnish each plate with 2 olives and Parmigiano-Reggiano shavings and serve immediately.

■ Pencil-thin asparagus do not usually require much peeling or trimming. However, if you can only find medium or large stalks, they must be trimmed to the tender point and the outer skin peeled off with a vegetable peeler or sharp knife.

■ To eliminate problems with digestion, wrap raw onions in a clean kitchen towel and twist to squeeze out the liquid. Chef Danko feels that it is the onion juice that causes unpleasant reactions.

GARY DANKO: *Asparagus with Red Onion Vinaigrette*

Roast Salmon with Moroccan Spices

SERVES 6
PREPARATION TIME: ABOUT 1 HOUR
COOKING TIME: ABOUT 45 MINUTES

This dish makes a dramatic and aromatic statement when it is presented at the table. As you cut open the foil wrapper, the sensual Moroccan spices waft out to enrapture your dinner guests. A tempting alternative to plain poached salmon, this can be served hot, cold, or at room temperature.

3 tablespoons chopped fresh cilantro
3 tablespoons chopped fresh flat-leaf parsley
1 1/2 tablespoons cumin seeds
1 tablespoon Hungarian paprika
1/2 teaspoon crumbled saffron threads
1 tablespoon coarse salt
1/4 cup extra-virgin olive oil
1 1/2 tablespoons fresh lemon juice
1 1/2 teaspoons harissa or Tabasco, or to taste
One 8-pound salmon, cleaned, head left on and fins and tail removed, rinsed, and patted dry
Special Equipment: Instant-read thermometer

1 Assemble *mise en place* trays for this recipe (see page 7).

2 Preheat the oven to 350 degrees F.

3 In a small bowl, combine the cilantro, parsley, cumin, paprika, saffron, and coarse salt. Whisk in the oil, lemon juice, and harissa. Generously coat the salmon on all sides with the spice mixture.

4 Center a sheet of heavy-duty aluminum foil 18 inches wide and 2 feet long, shiny side up, on a baking sheet large enough to hold the fish. Put the fish and any remaining marinade in the center of the foil. Cover with a matching sheet of foil. Fold up and tightly crimp the edges together to make an airtight packet.

5 Roast for about 45 minutes, or until an instant-read thermometer registers 140 degrees F when inserted through the foil into the thickest part of the fish. Remove and let rest for 5 minutes without opening the foil.

6 Transfer the entire packet to a serving platter and cut the foil open at the table. Lift off large pieces of fish and spoon the cooking juices over them as you serve.

NOTE: If you make this marinade, known as *chermoula*, in advance, do not add the saffron until the last minute, or the flavor will be lost.

■ Any large firm-fleshed fish, such as red snapper, can be substituted for the salmon.

Grain Pilaf

SERVES 6
PREPARATION TIME: ABOUT 15 MINUTES
COOKING TIME: FROM 4 TO 60 MINUTES, DEPENDING
ON GRAIN CHOSEN

Gary loves to experiment with grains. He frequently cooks a number of different ones and combines them to create a new taste—as well as an interesting side dish. For this pilaf, combine all four or only two of the suggested grains to serve with the salmon. To serve six people, you will need to start with about two cups of uncooked grain, so mix and match the grains accordingly. If you cook all four grains, you will have twice as much pilaf as you need, but it is delicious cold or reheated the next day.

MILLET:
2 tablespoons olive oil or unsalted butter
1/4 cup minced onion
1 cup millet
2 1/2 cups water
Coarse salt to taste

BULGUR OR QUINOA:
2 tablespoons olive oil or unsalted butter
1/4 cup minced onion
1 cup bulgur or well-washed quinoa
2 cups water
Coarse salt to taste

WEHANI RICE:

2 tablespoons olive oil or unsalted butter
1/4 cup minced onion
1 cup Wehani rice
3 cups water
Coarse salt to taste

COUSCOUS:

2 tablespoons olive oil or unsalted butter
1/4 cup minced onion
1 cup couscous
1 cup boiling water
Coarse salt to taste

1 Assemble *mise en place* trays for this recipe (see page 7).

2 To prepare the millet, in a medium-sized saucepan, heat the oil over medium heat. Add the onions and sauté for about 3 minutes, or until just softened. Stir in the millet and sauté for 1 minute. Add the water and coarse salt to taste and bring to a boil. Reduce the heat, cover, and just barely simmer for 15 to 20 minutes, or until tender. Remove from the heat and keep warm.

3 To prepare the bulgur or quinoa, in a medium-sized saucepan, heat the oil over medium heat. Add the onions

and sauté for 3 minutes, or until just softened. Stir in the grain and sauté for 1 minute. Add the water and coarse salt to taste and bring to a boil. Reduce the heat, cover, and just barely simmer for 15 minutes, or until tender. Remove from the heat and allow to rest for 5 minutes.

4 To prepare the rice, in a medium-sized saucepan, heat the oil over medium heat. Add the onions and sauté for about 3 minutes, or until just softened. Stir in the rice and sauté for 1 minute. Add the water and coarse salt to taste and bring to a boil. Reduce the heat, cover, and just barely simmer for 50 minutes, or until tender. Remove from the heat and keep warm.

5 To prepare the couscous, in a medium-sized saucepan, heat the oil over medium heat. Add the onions and sauté for about 3 minutes, or until just softened. Stir in the couscous and sauté for 15 seconds. Immediately add the boiling water and remove the pan from the heat. Cover and allow to rest for 5 minutes.

6 Fluff the grains with a fork before serving and combine.

■ Most grains can be kept warm, tightly covered, in a very low oven for up to 1 hour. You can also reheat them, tightly covered, in a 300-degree-F oven for about 20 minutes.

Gratin of Strawberries and Rhubarb with Warm Nutmeg Cream and Pistachio Ice Cream

SERVES 6
PREPARATION TIME: ABOUT 40 MINUTES
BAKING TIME: ABOUT 40 MINUTES
COOKING TIME: ABOUT 30 MINUTES
FREEZING TIME (ICE CREAM ONLY): ABOUT 24 HOURS

This gratin is a great addition to the traditional American combination of sweet spring strawberries and tart rhubarb. The pistachio ice cream adds a touch of Mediterranean flavor.

4 cups sliced strawberries
4 cups sliced rhubarb
1 cup granulated sugar
2 teaspoons ground cinnamon
1 1/2 teaspoons grated nutmeg
Pinch of ground cloves
1/8 teaspoon salt, plus a pinch
3/4 cup all-purpose flour

4 tablespoons unsalted butter, cubed and chilled
1/8 teaspoon grated lemon zest
Warm Nutmeg Cream (recipe follows)
Pistachio Ice Cream (recipe follows)
6 whole strawberries

1 Assemble *mise en place* trays for this recipe (see page 7).

2 Preheat the oven to 350 degrees F. Generously butter a shallow 2-quart baking dish.

3 In a large bowl, combine the strawberries, rhubarb, sugar, 1 1/2 teaspoons of the cinnamon, the nutmeg, cloves, and pinch of salt and toss well. Transfer to the baking dish.

4 In a food processor fitted with the metal blade, combine the flour, butter, lemon zest and the remaining 1/2 teaspoon cinnamon and 1/8 teaspoon salt. Process, using quick on and off pulses, until the texture is sandy.

5 Sprinkle the cinnamon topping over the fruit and bake for about 40 minutes, or until bubbling and golden brown. Cool for about 10 minutes before serving.

6 Spoon the gratin onto 6 warm dessert plates. Spoon some Warm Nutmeg Cream on top and place a scoop of Pistachio Ice Cream at the side of each serving. Garnish each plate with a whole strawberry and serve immediately.

WARM NUTMEG CREAM
MAKES ABOUT 2 CUPS

2 cups heavy cream
1/2 cup granulated sugar
8 tablespoons (1 stick) unsalted butter
1/4 teaspoon grated nutmeg
Pinch of salt

In a small nonstick saucepan, combine the cream, sugar, butter, nutmeg, and salt and bring to a boil over medium heat. Reduce the heat and simmer, stirring occasionally, for about 10 minutes, or until the mixture thickens enough to coat the back of a spoon. Serve warm.

GARY DANKO: *Gratin of Strawberries and Rhubarb with Warm Nutmeg Cream and Pistachio Ice Cream*

PISTACHIO ICE CREAM
MAKES ABOUT 2 QUARTS

1/4 cup plus 2 tablespoons chopped pistachios
1 cup plus 1 tablespoon granulated sugar
1/4 teaspoon grated lemon zest
Pinch of ground green cardamom
1/4 teaspoon salt, plus a pinch
1 large egg white
3 cups heavy cream
1 1/2 cups milk
1/2 vanilla bean, split
10 large egg yolks

■ **Special Equipment:** Ice cream freezer

1 In a food processor fitted with the metal blade, combine the pistachios, 3 tablespoons of the sugar, the lemon zest, cardamom, and pinch of salt. Process until the pistachios are coarsely ground. Add the egg white and process to a fine paste. Transfer to a bowl and set aside.

2 In a medium-sized saucepan, combine 1 1/2 cups of the heavy cream with the milk, vanilla bean, and the remaining 1/4 teaspoon salt and bring to a boil over high heat. Immediately remove from the heat and set aside.

3 In a heavy medium-sized saucepan, whisk together the egg yolks, pistachio paste, and the remaining 3/4 cup plus 2 tablespoons sugar. Whisking constantly, blend in a bit of the hot cream to temper the eggs. Set over medium heat and whisk in the remaining hot cream. Cook, stirring constantly, for about 15 minutes, or until the mixture thickens enough to coat the back of the spoon. Whisk in the remaining 1 1/2 cups cream and remove from the heat. Remove the vanilla bean. Let the mixture cool to room temperature and then refrigerate until chilled. Or chill the mixture in an ice water bath.

4 Pour into an ice cream freezer and freeze according to the manufacturer's directions. When frozen, transfer to a 2-quart container with a tight-fitting lid. Cover and freeze for at least 24 hours before serving.

NOTE: You can make the pistachio paste as coarse or fine as you like. If you want an absolutely smooth texture to the ice cream, strain the cream mixture through a fine sieve before pouring into the ice cream freezer.

TRIBUTE TO THE SOUTH OF FRANCE

Warm Shrimp Salad
with Crisp Marinated Vegetables

St. Pierre Roasted on a Bed of Fennel
with Fresh Tomato Purée and Niçoise Olives

Sautéed Pears with Honey Ice Cream

WINE SUGGESTIONS:
Chardonnay or White Côtes-du-Rhône *(first course)*
Pinot Grigio or Sauvignon Blanc *(second course)*
Tawny Port *(dessert)*

WHAT YOU CAN PREPARE AHEAD OF TIME

Up to 1 week ahead: Make the Honey Ice Cream.

Early in the day: Prepare the vegetables for the Warm Shrimp Salad. Place in plastic bags and refrigerate. Make the tomato puree and prepare the basil and olives for the St. Pierre Roasted on a Bed of Fennel. Cover and refrigerate. Sauté the pears for the dessert (undercook them slightly, cover, and refrigerate). Reheat before serving.

Just a mention of the world-renowned Alain Ducasse brings a smile to my face. Currently, he is the only chef in a hotel to have three Michelin stars—for the extraordinary Louis XV Restaurant in Monte Carlo. I met Alain many years ago in New York while he was the executive chef at the Hotel Terrasse in Juan-les-Pins. He asked to teach at De Gustibus, a request I was reluctant to encourage, as he spoke no English. But, of course, he convinced me and an incredible class resulted. Even though most of us there spoke no French, the passion and love he brought to the classroom transcended all boundaries. We were enthralled.

Alain Ducasse is best known for his ardor for the fresh, near-perfect ingredients found in the South of France and for the simple but simply delicious preparations to which they lend themselves. He always maximizes basic flavor and frequently does little to alter the inherent taste of his ingredients. In the years since we first met and he mesmerized the De Gustibus classroom, I have had the good fortune to dine several times at Louis XV. Each time I am dazzled by his talents. Vive le Chef Ducasse!

◁ ALAIN DUCASSE: *Warm Shrimp Salad with Crisp Marinated Vegetables*

Warm Shrimp Salad with Crisp Marinated Vegetables

SERVES 6
PREPARATION TIME: ABOUT 30 MINUTES
COOKING TIME: ABOUT 3 MINUTES

This dish embodies everything great food should be; it's light, colorful, and filled with flavor. You must have absolutely peak-of-freshness vegetables for it to be perfect.

1/2 pound pencil-thin asparagus, trimmed, stalks finely minced and tips reserved
1/2 pound very ripe tomatoes, peeled, cored, seeded, finely diced, and drained
2/3 pound very young fava beans, shelled and peeled, or baby lima beans, shelled
4 baby artichoke hearts, finely diced (see Note)
1/2 cup plus 1 tablespoon extra-virgin olive oil
Juice of 1/2 lemon
Coarse salt and freshly ground black pepper to taste
2 pounds peeled and deveined medium-sized shrimp (2 1/2 to 3 pounds shrimp in the shell)
1 cup shredded fresh basil

1 Assemble *mise en place* trays for this recipe (see page 7).

2 In a nonreactive bowl, combine the asparagus, tomatoes, beans, and artichokes. Add 1/2 cup of the oil, the lemon juice, and coarse salt and pepper to taste. Toss and let marinate for about 5 minutes.

3 In a large sauté pan, heat the remaining 1 tablespoon oil over medium-high heat. Add the shrimp, season to taste with coarse salt and pepper, and sauté for about 3 minutes, or until pink and just opaque throughout. Remove from the heat.

4 Place equal portions of the marinated vegetables on each plate. Top with the shrimp and garnish with the shredded basil. Serve immediately.

NOTE: For baby artichoke hearts, buy tiny artichokes and peel away only the tough outer leaves. If the choke is tough, cut it away. Very often, in very small artichokes the choke may be tender enough to eat.

■ If any of the vegetables are not available in their pristine state, replace them with those that are.

St. Pierre Roasted on a Bed of Fennel with Fresh Tomato Purée and Niçoise Olives

SERVES 6
PREPARATION TIME: ABOUT 30 MINUTES
COOKING TIME: ABOUT 20 MINUTES

Here again, the flavor of the dish depends on the quality of the ingredients. Each should be at the height of its goodness—the fish fresh from the sea, the tomatoes picked from the vine, and the basil snipped from its stalk—and the olive oil and olives of the finest quality.

2 pounds very ripe tomatoes, peeled, cored, seeded, and diced
Three 2 1/2- to 3-pound St. Pierre (John Dory) or red snapper, well cleaned, heads removed
Coarse salt and freshly ground black pepper to taste
1/4 pound dried fennel twigs (see Note)
1/2 cup water
1/2 cup extra-virgin olive oil
8 tablespoons (1 stick) unsalted butter, softened
Juice of 1/2 lemon

1/2 cup pitted and quartered Niçoise olives
3 tablespoons minced fresh basil
1 tablespoon slivered fresh basil

1 Assemble *mise en place* trays for this recipe (see page 7).

2 Preheat the oven to 400 degrees F.

3 In a food processor fitted with the metal blade, process the tomatoes until smooth. Transfer to a fine sieve lined with cheesecloth and allow to drain thoroughly, then transfer to a medium-sized nonstick sauté pan and set aside. (Reserve the juice for another use.)

ALAIN DUCASSE: *St. Pierre Roasted on a Bed of Fennel with Fresh Tomato Purée and Niçoise Olives (red snapper substituted in photograph)* ▷

4 Pat the fish dry and season to taste with coarse salt and pepper. Put the fennel twigs in a baking dish large enough to hold the fish comfortably. Add the water and set the fish on the twigs. Sprinkle with 6 tablespoons of the oil and tightly cover with aluminum foil.

5 Bake for about 15 minutes, or just until the fish flakes when pierced with a fork and the flesh is opaque throughout. Transfer to a warm serving dish and cover loosely to keep warm.

6 Strain the pan juices into a small saucepan and place over medium heat. Whisk in the butter, bit by bit. Whisk in the remaining 2 tablespoons oil. When well blended, whisk in the lemon juice and season to taste with coarse salt and pepper. Remove from the heat and keep warm.

7 Set the tomato purée over medium heat and add the olives and minced basil. Stir and cook for 2 minutes, or until just warm.

8 Lift the fillets from the fish and place 1 on each plate. Spoon a little tomato purée around the fish. Add the slivered basil to the butter sauce, stir gently, and spoon on either side of the fish. Serve immediately.

NOTE: Dried fennel twigs are available at specialty stores. One large bunch of basil should be sufficient for this recipe.

■ You can replace the St. Pierre with any other firm-textured, nonfatty fish, such as striped bass or black sea bass. If whole fish are not available, use 6 fillets about 1 inch thick.

Sautéed Pears with Honey Ice Cream

SERVES 6
PREPARATION TIME: ABOUT 20 MINUTES
COOKING TIME: ABOUT 10 MINUTES
FREEZING TIME (ICE CREAM ONLY): ABOUT 7 HOURS

The honey ice cream brings a full-bodied taste of the Mediterranean to this dessert. Use pears or choose another seasonally ripe fruit (apples or nectarines, for example) that complements the honey flavor.

2 cups milk
1 cup heavy cream
4 large egg yolks
1 cup honey
8 tablespoons (1 stick) unsalted butter
4 Bartlett or other firm pears, peeled, cored, halved, and sliced
¼ cup granulated sugar

■ **Special Equipment:** Ice cream freezer

1 Assemble *mise en place* trays for this recipe (see page 7).

2 Pour the milk into a medium-sized saucepan and the cream into a small saucepan. Bring each to a boil over medium heat, remove from the heat, and immediately pour the cream into the milk.

3 In a small bowl, whisk the egg yolks and honey together. Whisk in a bit of the hot milk mixture to temper the eggs and then whisk the eggs into the milk mixture. Return to medium heat and, whisking constantly, bring to a simmer. Cook for 2 minutes, whisking constantly, or until the mixture thickens enough to coat the back of a spoon. Cool to room temperature and then refrigerate until chilled. Or chill in an ice water bath.

4 Strain the mixture through a fine sieve into an ice cream freezer. Freeze according to the manufacturer's directions. When frozen, transfer to a container with a tight-fitting lid. Cover and freeze for at least 6 hours before serving.

5 In a large sauté pan, melt the butter over medium heat. Add the pears and sugar and sauté for about 5 minutes, or until golden. Place an equal portion in each shallow bowl and top with a scoop of ice cream. Serve immediately.

◁ ALAIN DUCASSE: *Sautéed Pears with Honey Ice Cream*

WINNING COMBINATIONS

Fig and Prosciutto Tart

*Grilled and Chilled Salmon Salad
with Artichoke Guacamole*

Chocolate Risotto Pudding

WINE SUGGESTIONS:

Prosecco (Italian sparkling wine) *(first course)*

Sauvignon Blanc or Pinot Blanc *(second course)*

WHAT YOU CAN PREPARE AHEAD OF TIME

Up to 1 week ahead: Make and freeze the pizza dough for the Fig and Prosciutto Tart. Make the fig jam for the tart. Cover and refrigerate.

Up to 2 days ahead: Cook and cut up the artichokes for the Artichoke Guacamole. Cover and refrigerate.

Up to 1 day ahead: Make the pizza dough for the Fig and Prosciutto Tart, if not already made. Marinate the salmon for the Grilled and Chilled Salmon Salad. Make the Artichoke Guacamole.

Early in the day: Grill the salmon. Fry the artichoke leaves. Plump the raisins for the Chocolate Risotto Pudding if using.

Todd English is a dynamic young American chef whose heart has a direct link to the Mediterranean. He adores the foods and the atmosphere of the region so much that he named his two Boston-area restaurants Olives and Figs: a clear reference to the foods of southern France, Spain, Italy, and Greece. Todd particularly likes to work with classical culinary combinations, which he recreates in inventive juxtapositions. He is an exciting chef, full of energy and respect for his ingredients, with genuine skill at layering flavors in complex ways. The De Gustibus students enjoy his enthusiasm and the intoxicating quality of his dishes. In the recipes Chef English prepared for this class, his sense of humor and skill at playing with the classics absolutely shine. The following menu is most appropriate for casual entertaining or a buffet dinner.

◁ TODD ENGLISH: *Fig and Prosciutto Tart* and *Grilled and Chilled Salmon Salad with Artichoke Guacamole*

Fig and Prosciutto Tart

Todd told us that the combination of fresh figs and prosciutto was one of his most favorite childhood treats. Memories of his Italian boyhood helped create this unusual tart, combining the always-available sweet, dried figs with salty prosciutto, slightly pungent Gorgonzola, and rich pizza dough.

1/2 cup red wine
1 cup balsamic vinegar
2/3 cup granulated sugar
1 cup roughly chopped dried figs, preferably Turkish
3 sprigs fresh rosemary, leaves only, chopped
Pizza Dough (recipe follows)
3 tablespoons olive oil
1/4 cup crumbled Gorgonzola cheese
12 to 18 thin slices prosciutto

■ Special Equipment: Pizza stone or baking tiles

1 Assemble *mise en place* trays for this recipe (see page 7).

2 In a medium-sized nonreactive saucepan, bring the wine to a boil over high heat. Reduce the heat and simmer gently for about 7 minutes, or until reduced by half. Raise the heat, add the vinegar, and bring to a boil. Reduce the heat and simmer for about 15 minutes, or until reduced by half. Stir in the sugar, adjust the heat so that the mixture just barely simmers, and cook, stirring frequently, for 5 minutes. Add the figs and half the rosemary and cook, stirring frequently, for about 20 minutes, or until the figs are plump and the jam has thickened. Allow to cool to room temperature.

3 Set a pizza stone or baking tiles on the bottom rack and preheat the oven to 450 degrees F.

4 Divide the dough into 6 equal portions. Working with one piece at a time, on a lightly floured surface, roll out each portion into a 1/2-inch-thick circle about 8 inches in diameter. Drizzle each circle with 1 1/2 teaspoons oil, sprinkle with the remaining rosemary, and spread a thin layer of fig jam over each. Sprinkle the Gorgonzola over the jam. Crimp the edges of the tarts by folding small pinches of dough in toward the center.

5 Place the tarts on the hot stone and bake for about 15 minutes, or until the crust is lightly browned and crisp and the cheese has melted. Remove from the oven and lay 2 to 3 pieces of prosciutto on top of each. Serve immediately.

NOTE: If your baking stone and oven are large enough, bake all the pizzas at once. Otherwise, bake 2 to 3 at a time and serve immediately, or cover to keep warm until all are baked.

■ If fresh figs are in season, Chef English recommends placing a few slices on top of the prosciutto for garnish.

■ The fig jam also makes a rich condiment for grilled or roasted pork or duck.

TODD ENGLISH: *Fig and Prosciutto Tart*

PIZZA DOUGH

MAKES SIX 8-INCH ROUND PIZZAS OR 2 MEDIUM-SIZED PIZZAS

1½ teaspoons active dry yeast
1½ teaspoons honey
2 cups lukewarm water
2 tablespoons olive oil
2 cups all-purpose flour
½ teaspoon salt
8 tablespoons (1 stick) unsalted butter, softened

1 In a large bowl, combine the yeast, honey, and ½ cup of the water. Let stand for 5 minutes, or until the mixture bubbles and swells. Stir in the oil and the remaining 1½ cups water with a wooden spoon. Stir in the flour and salt until well combined.

2 Turn the dough out onto a lightly floured surface and knead for about 10 minutes, or until elastic and smooth. Form into a ball and place in a lightly oiled bowl, turning the dough to coat it with oil. Cover loosely and place in a warm spot for about 1 hour, or until doubled in size.

3 Turn the dough out onto a lightly floured surface and flatten it into a smooth, even rectangle about 6 inches wide and 10 inches long. Using a spatula, spread the butter over one half of the rectangle. Fold the dough in half, like a book, to cover the butter and flatten with a rolling pin into a rectangle about 6 inches wide and 10 inches long. Fold and roll out three more times, turning the folded dough a quarter turn between each rolling. Wrap in plastic wrap and refrigerate for 1 hour.

4 Divide the dough into 6 pieces and follow the recipe for the tart, beginning with step 4.

NOTE: To freeze the dough, divide it into the desired number of pieces, roll out to pizza shapes, and wrap tightly in plastic wrap and foil. It is not necessary to thaw the dough before topping and baking, but it may require a longer baking time.

■ This recipe can be used to make larger pizzas than called for in the tart recipe.

Grilled and Chilled Salmon Salad with Artichoke Guacamole

SERVES 6
PREPARATION TIME: ABOUT 1 HOUR
MARINATING TIME (SALMON ONLY): 1 TO 24 HOURS
COOKING TIME: ABOUT 1 HOUR AND 15 MINUTES

Artichoke bottoms replace the avocado and the sesame oil adds an unexpected dimension to this unusual "guacamole," served with a chilled salmon salad. Although this is a rather involved recipe, so much can be done in advance that it is not as difficult as it as first seems.

3 tablespoons chopped fresh thyme
1 clove garlic, finely minced
½ cup olive oil
1 pound skinless, boneless salmon fillet
6 large artichokes, stems and tough outer leaves removed
2 lemons, halved
2 cups milk
1 ripe tomato, cored, seeded, and diced
¼ cup finely diced red onion
1 teaspoon dark Asian sesame oil
Salt and freshly ground black pepper to taste
3 tablespoons balsamic vinegar

2 tablespoons Dijon mustard
1 tablespoon minced shallots
1 cup Japanese bread crumbs (*panko*) or other crisp bread crumbs
Vegetable oil
1 bunch fresh chervil, snipped into tiny sprigs

1 Prepare *mise en place* trays for this recipe (see page 7).

2 In a small shallow nonreactive baking dish, combine the thyme and garlic with 2 tablespoons of the olive oil. Place the salmon in the mixture and turn to coat both sides. Cover and refrigerate for at least 1 hour, or up to 24 hours.

3 In a large nonreactive pot, cover the artichokes with water. Squeeze the juice of 3 of the lemon halves into the pot and then add the 3 lemon halves. Cover and bring to a boil over medium-high heat. Reduce the heat and simmer for 45 minutes, or until the outer leaves come loose with a

TODD ENGLISH: *Grilled and Chilled Salmon Salad with Artichoke Guacamole*

slight tug. Drain and place upside down on paper towels to cool.

4 When cool, remove and discard the outer layer of artichoke leaves. Remove the remaining leaves from the artichokes until you reach the very small tender leaves (take care to avoid the sharp thorns on the tips). Place 36 to 42 of the largest leaves in a shallow container, add the milk, cover, and refrigerate until ready to use.

5 Using a sharp knife, remove and discard the small leaves and the hairy choke of the artichokes to expose the meaty bottoms. Cut the bottoms into 1/4-inch dice and put in a small bowl. Gently fold in the tomatoes, onions, and sesame oil. Squeeze in the juice from the remaining lemon half and season to taste with salt and pepper. Stir gently, cover, and set aside.

6 In a small bowl, whisk together the vinegar and mustard. Slowly add the remaining 6 tablespoons olive oil, whisking constantly until emulsified. Stir in the shallots and set aside.

7 Prepare a charcoal or gas grill or preheat the broiler.

8 Grill the salmon for about 8 minutes, turning once, or until just barely cooked in the center. Set aside.

9 Put the bread crumbs in a large plastic bag and set aside.

10 Pour vegetable oil into a large deep heavy frying pan to a depth of about 2 inches and heat over high heat until very hot but not smoking. A few at a time, remove the artichoke leaves from the milk and put in the bag with the bread crumbs, tossing to coat. Shake off the excess crumbs and fry the leaves for about 1 minute, or until golden. Drain on paper towels. Repeat with the remaining leaves.

11 Place a dollop of the artichoke "guacamole" on the wide end of each fried artichoke leaf. Flake about 1 tablespoon of salmon on top and garnish with a tiny sprig of chervil. Serve immediately.

Chocolate Risotto Pudding

Both chocolate and rice pudding are desserts fraught with nostalgia. Todd took these childhood memories and created an entirely new dessert with a very grown-up taste.

6 cups water
1 cup milk
2 large egg yolks
1/2 cup nonalkalized cocoa powder
1/4 cup granulated sugar
1 tablespoon unsalted butter
1 1/2 cups Arborio rice
1 vanilla bean, split lengthwise
Grated zest and juice of 1 small orange
5 ounces semisweet chocolate, coarsely chopped
1/2 cup raisins, plumped in 1/2 cup orange liqueur, such as Grand Marnier (optional)
1/2 cup chopped toasted walnuts
3 small fresh mint sprigs

1 Assemble *mise en place* trays for this recipe (see page 7).

2 In a medium-sized saucepan, bring the water to a boil over high heat. Reduce the heat so the water continues to boil gently.

3 In a medium-sized bowl, whisk together the milk, egg yolks, cocoa, and sugar until very smooth. Set aside.

4 In a heavy-bottomed straight-sided medium-sized saucepan, melt the butter over medium heat. Add the rice and stir to coat. Ladle in just enough boiling water to cover the rice, add the vanilla bean, and cook, stirring, until all the liquid has been absorbed by the rice. Continue stirring and adding water, about 1 cup at a time, until all the water is absorbed or the rice is *al dente*—whichever happens first. This should take no more than 20 to 25 minutes.

5 Stir the milk mixture into the rice. Add the orange zest and juice and cook, stirring constantly, for about 6 minutes, or until the mixture is the consistency of custard (although it will not be as smooth because of the rice). Add the chocolate and cook, stirring constantly, for about 2 minutes, or until it has melted. Remove from the heat. Remove the vanilla bean, stir in the raisins, if using, and

any liquid. Pour into a warm serving bowl, sprinkle with the nuts, and garnish with the mint sprigs. Serve immediately.

NOTE: Although this pudding is best served warm, it can also be served at room temperature or chilled.

TODD ENGLISH: *Chocolate Risotto Pudding*

59

VIBRANT SPANISH TASTES

*Baked Eggplant and Manchego Salad
with Oregano and Balsamic Vinegar Glaze*

*Flatbread with Spicy Hummus, Goat Cheese,
and Roasted Vegetables*

*Roasted Pork Tenderloin with Tapenade
and Charred Yellow Pepper Sauce*

Bolo Apple Cake

WINE SUGGESTIONS:

White Rioja, Rias Baixas, or Cava (Sparkling wine from Spain)
(first course—eggplant salad and flatbread)

Spanish Red such as Ribera del Duero or Young Rioja *(second course)*

Tawny Port *(dessert)*

WHAT YOU CAN PREPARE AHEAD OF TIME

Up to 3 days ahead: Prepare the Tapenade and Yellow Pepper Sauce for the Roasted Pork Tenderloin. Cover and refrigerate.

Up to 1 day ahead: Assemble the eggplant stacks for the Oven-Baked Eggplant. Cover and refrigerate. Before serving, bake according to the recipe instructions. Prepare the glaze for the eggplant. Bake the Flatbread and prepare the Spicy Hummus. Cover and refrigerate the hummus. Bring to room temperature before serving.

Early in the day: Roast the vegetables for the Flatbread, cover, and refrigerate. Stuff the Roasted Pork Tenderloin. Cover and refrigerate. Bake the Bolo Apple Cake. Before serving, heat the cake in a preheated 300-degree-F oven for about 7 minutes if desired.

Whenever Bobby Flay teaches at De Gustibus, the crowds follow. That is in part because this talented young chef is always ready to experience and share a new adventure. When he opened Mesa Grill, the perennially *hot* New York City restaurant, it was to introduce diners to his interpretation of Southwestern food. With Bobby's great palate and classical training at the French Culinary Institute, the restaurant was an instant success. This led him to dreams of authentic Spanish flavors and the desire to explore the colorfully robust foods of that country. With his partner, Laurence Kretchmer, Bobby opened Bolo, a vibrant eating spot featuring his intrinsic definition of the cuisine of Spain. Although the menu is not a classical one, it captures the spirit and flavor of the Mediterranean.

◁ **BOBBY FLAY:** *Flatbread with Spicy Hummus, Goat Cheese, and Roasted Vegetables* **and** *Baked Eggplant and Manchego Salad with Oregano and Balsamic Vinegar Glaze*

Baked Eggplant and Manchego Salad with Oregano and Balsamic Vinegar Glaze

Although this dish is an inspired first course, it would also make a terrific vegetarian main course. The meltingly mellow sheep's milk cheese adds an authentic taste of Spain.

8 medium-sized eggplants, peeled and sliced crosswise 1/8 inch thick (5 to 6 pounds total; see Note)
1/4 cup olive oil
2 cups balsamic vinegar
1/2 pound Manchego cheese, sliced paper-thin
1 cup loosely packed fresh oregano leaves
Salt and freshly ground black pepper to taste
About 1 teaspoon ancho chile powder or Spanish paprika

1 Assemble *mise en place* trays for this recipe (see page 7).

2 Preheat the oven to 425 degrees F.

3 Lay the eggplant slices in a single layer on ungreased baking sheets. Using a pastry brush, lightly coat both sides with oil. Bake for about 8 minutes, or until slightly softened but not mushy. Allow to cool on the baking sheets. (Do not turn the oven off.)

4 In a small nonreactive saucepan, bring the vinegar to a boil over high heat. Reduce the heat slightly and simmer for about 10 minutes, or until the vinegar turns syrupy. Cool slightly, transfer to a plastic squeeze bottle with a fine tip, and set aside.

5 Lay a slice of cheese on a slice of eggplant, sprinkle with a few oregano leaves, and season to taste with salt and pepper. Continue making layers in this manner, using 6 slices of eggplant in all. Sprinkle the top slice with chile powder. Transfer to a nonstick baking sheet. Make 5 more identical stacks. Bake for about 10 minutes.

6 Cut each eggplant stack in half on the diagonal and set one stack on each plate, separating the halves slightly. Drizzle each with the balsamic glaze and sprinkle with a few oregano leaves. Serve immediately.

NOTE: As many as 8 eggplants are needed to get 36 uniformly sized slices. Discard the tapered ends, or use them for another dish.

Flatbread with Spicy Hummus, Goat Cheese, and Roasted Vegetables

The flavors absolutely blossom on this multileveled pizza-like appetizer. I could easily eat it as light lunch or supper.

2 medium-sized eggplants, trimmed and quartered
2 red bell peppers, cored, seeded, and quartered
2 yellow bell peppers, cored, seeded, and quartered
1 large red onion, quartered
8 spears asparagus, trimmed
1/4 cup plus 1 tablespoon olive oil
Salt and freshly ground black pepper to taste
3 cups drained cooked chickpeas
1/4 cup tahini

1/4 cup chopped fresh flat-leaf parsley
2 tablespoons chopped garlic
2 teaspoons minced green *chile de árbol* or other hot green chile
1/4 cup fresh lemon juice
1 tablespoon honey
1 tablespoon ground cumin
Flatbread (recipe follows)
1/4 cup crumbled fresh goat cheese
1/4 cup pitted black olives
1/4 cup Basil Oil (recipe follows; optional)

■ Special Equipment: Pizza stone or baking tiles

1 Assemble *mise en place* trays for this recipe (see page 7).

2 Preheat the oven to 400 degrees F.

3 Toss the eggplant, peppers, onions, and asparagus with 3 tablespoons of the olive oil and season with salt and pepper to taste. Arrange on nonstick baking sheets, keeping the vegetables separate, and bake until just tender and slightly crisp, turning occasionally, about 10 minutes for the asparagus, 15 minutes for the eggplant, 20 minutes for the peppers, and 25 minutes for the onions. Set aside. When the peppers are cool, peel off the skin with a sharp knife. Increase the oven temperature to 450 degrees F and place a pizza stone or baking tiles on the bottom rack.

4 In a food processor fitted with the metal blade, combine the chickpeas, tahini, parsley, garlic, chile, lemon juice, the remaining 2 tablespoons olive oil, the honey, cumin, and salt and pepper to taste. Process until the chickpeas are finely chopped but the mixture is not smoothly puréed.

5 Spread the hummus on the flatbread and top with an assortment of roasted vegetables. Sprinkle with the goat cheese. Place on the pizza stone and bake for about 5 minutes, or until the cheese is melting and the flatbread is hot. Garnish with olives and, if desired, drizzle Basil Oil over the top. Serve immediately.

NOTE: If your baking stone is large enough, bake all the flatbreads at once. Otherwise, bake 2 to 3 at a time and serve immediately, or cover to keep warm until all are baked.

FLATBREAD
MAKES 6

1¼ cups lukewarm water
3 tablespoons olive oil
1½ teaspoons granulated sugar
½ ounce fresh yeast or 1 package (¼ ounce) active dry yeast
¾ cup buckwheat flour
1½ tablespoons salt
About 3 cups sifted bread flour

■ Special Equipment: Electric mixer with dough hook

1 In the bowl of an electric mixer fitted with a dough hook, combine the water, 2 tablespoons of the oil, the sugar, and yeast. Mix on low speed for about 1 minute, or

until the sugar and yeast are dissolved. Add the buckwheat flour and salt. Add the bread flour ¼ cup at a time, mixing until the dough forms a cohesive mass. Turn the dough out onto a lightly floured surface and divide into 6 pieces. Form each piece into a ball, place the balls on a nonstick baking sheet, and lightly brush with the remaining 1 tablespoon oil. Cover loosely and set aside in a warm place to rise for 2 hours, until nearly doubled in volume.

2 Preheat the oven to 450 degrees F and place a pizza stone or baking tiles on the lower rack.

3 Pat the balls into discs. On a lightly floured surface, sprinkle each disc with flour and roll out to a circle about ⅛ inch thick. Prick the circles all over with a fork, place on the pizza stone, and bake for about 5 minutes, or until crisp and browned around the edges. Serve warm or cool.

NOTE: You can make the dough ahead of time, form it into balls, and let them rise in the refrigerator for up to 12 hours.

BASIL OIL
MAKES ABOUT 2 CUPS

1½ cups fresh basil leaves
1 cup olive oil
Salt and freshly ground black pepper to taste

1 In a small saucepan of boiling water, blanch the basil leaves for about 10 seconds. Immediately drain and rinse under cold running water. Squeeze dry.

2 In a food processor fitted with the metal blade, combine the basil, oil, and salt and pepper to taste and process until smooth. Strain the oil through a fine sieve. Transfer to a nonreactive container and refrigerate for up to 1 week.

NOTE: The flavor will fade as the oil stands. You can store the oil in a plastic squeeze bottle with a fine tip so it will be ready to drizzle as an accent on any number of finished dishes.

Roasted Pork Tenderloins with Tapenade and Charred Yellow Pepper Sauce

SERVES 6
PREPARATION TIME: ABOUT 30 MINUTES
COOKING TIME: ABOUT 20 MINUTES

This is guaranteed to be an "in-demand" dinner party recipe. The flavors blend together beautifully, the colors are stupendous, and every part of the dish can be done in advance. Plus, it tastes just as good served at room temperature.

3 pork tenderloins, about 1 pound each
1/2 cup plus 1 tablespoon Black Olive Tapenade (recipe follows)
2 tablespoons Spanish paprika
Salt and freshly ground black pepper to taste
1/4 cup olive oil
1 1/2 cups Charred Yellow Pepper Sauce (recipe follows)

BOBBY FLAY: *Roasted Pork Tenderloins with Tapenade and Charred Yellow Pepper Sauce*

1 Assemble *mise en place* trays for this recipe (see page 7).

2 Preheat the oven to 350 degrees F.

3 Using a very sharp knife, make a lengthwise cut along the side of 1 tenderloin, taking care not to cut all the way through. Gently push the tenderloin open to butterfly it. Spread 3 tablespoons of the tapenade down the length of the opening, fold the meat over into its original shape, and tie closed with kitchen twine. Season liberally with the paprika and salt and pepper. Repeat with the remaining tenderloins.

4 In a large sauté pan, heat the oil over medium-high heat. Add the loins and sear for about 5 minutes, or until lightly browned on all sides. Transfer to a rimmed baking sheet or roasting pan and roast for about 12 minutes, or until just cooked through (and the internal temperature reaches 160 degrees F). Allow to rest for 5 minutes.

5 Cut the tenderloin crosswise into 1/2-inch-thick slices and arrange down the center of a serving platter. Serve with the Charred Yellow Pepper Sauce.

BLACK OLIVE TAPENADE
MAKES ABOUT 1 1/2 CUPS

1 cup pitted black olives
2 anchovy fillets
1 tablespoon minced garlic
1 tablespoon pine nuts
2 tablespoons fresh lemon juice
2 tablespoons olive oil
Salt and freshly ground black pepper to taste

In a blender or a food processor fitted with the metal blade, combine the olives, anchovies, garlic, pine nuts, lemon juice, and oil. Process until well blended but still textured (not as smooth as a purée). Season to taste with salt and pepper. Transfer to a nonreactive container, cover, and refrigerate until ready to use.

■ Use your favorite brine- or oil-cured black olives for the tapenade.

CHARRED YELLOW PEPPER SAUCE
MAKES ABOUT 2½ CUPS

2 roasted yellow bell peppers, peeled, cored, and seeded
2 shallots, chopped
⅓ cup sherry wine vinegar
1 teaspoon Spanish paprika
1 cup olive oil
Salt and freshly ground black pepper to taste

In a food processor fitted with the metal blade, combine the peppers, shallots, vinegar, and paprika. Process until smooth. With the machine running, slowly add the oil. When well emulsified, season to taste with salt and pepper. Transfer to a nonreactive container and refrigerate until ready to use.

Bolo Apple Cake

MAKES ONE 9-INCH ROUND CAKE
PREPARATION TIME: ABOUT 20 MINUTES
BAKING TIME: ABOUT 45 MINUTES

The flavor of sherry creates an intriguing note and gives a touch of the Spanish palate to this dessert.

3 large Granny Smith or other tart apples, peeled, cored, and cut into wedges
¾ cup lightly packed dark brown sugar
2 teaspoons cornstarch
½ cup plus 1 tablespoon dry sherry
2 teaspoons pure vanilla extract
¾ cup cake flour
½ teaspoon baking powder
¼ teaspoon baking soda
Pinch of salt
4 tablespoons unsalted butter, at room temperature
⅓ cup granulated sugar
1 large egg
¼ cup plus 2 tablespoons buttermilk, at room temperature

1 Assemble *mise en place* trays for this recipe (see page 7).

2 Preheat the oven to 400 degrees F.

3 Put the apples in a 2-quart baking dish. In a medium bowl, whisk together the brown sugar, cornstarch, ½ cup of the sherry, and 1 teaspoon of the vanilla. Pour over the apples and toss to coat. Bake, stirring occasionally, for about 25 minutes, or until the apples are slightly softened and beginning to brown. Remove from the oven, but do not turn off the oven.

4 Sift the flour, baking powder, baking soda, and salt together 3 times. Set aside.

5 In a large bowl, using an electric mixer set on medium-high speed, beat the butter and granulated sugar together for about 5 minutes, or until light and fluffy. Add the egg

and beat just until blended. Using a spatula, fold in a third of the flour mixture. Fold in half of the buttermilk and the remaining 1 tablespoon sherry and 1 teaspoon vanilla. Fold in another third of the flour mixture and then the remaining buttermilk. Fold in the remaining flour mixture.

6 Scrape the batter over the warm apples and smooth the top to cover the fruit. Bake for about 20 minutes, or until the cake is golden on top and the center springs back when lightly pressed. Serve warm.

■ The apples can be replaced by pears.

BOBBY FLAY: *Bolo Apple Cake*

CALIFORNIA ON THE MEDITERRANEAN

Spanish Fish Soup
CALDO DE PERRO

*Spaghetti with Saffroned Onions, Greens, Fennel,
Sun-Dried Tomatoes, and Currants*

Gateau Rolla

WINE SUGGESTIONS:

Sparkling California Wine, Spanish Cava, or White Sangria *(first course)*

Pinot Grigio *(second course)*

WHAT YOU CAN PREPARE AHEAD OF TIME

Up to 3 days ahead: Prepare the Fish Stock (if making your own). Make the Gateau Rolla.

Early in the day: Prepare the vegetables and citrus juices for the Spanish Fish Soup. Cover and refrigerate. Prepare the Aïoli. Prepare the vegetables for the Spaghetti with Saffroned Onions. Cover and refrigerate.

Joyce Goldstein is the grand doyenne of Mediterranean cuisine in America. The menu at her San Francisco restaurant, Square One, has evolved from her love of these robust foods, further refined by the personal touch she brings to everything she has accomplished. Because of her enthusiasm and precision, her classes at De Gustibus are always met with great anticipation. Joyce's articulate manner clearly defines her recipes; the hows and whys of each dish are readily understood by the home cook. Each of two main dishes presented here can easily stand alone. Serve either one with a green salad, a cheese course, and a great bottle of wine and you will have created a wonderful meal.

◁ JOYCE GOLDSTEIN: *Spanish Fish Soup*

Spanish Fish Soup

Caldo de Perro

The classic *caldo de perro* from Cadiz is made with only fish, fish stock, and the juice of bitter oranges. Joyce is a bit more expansive in her interpretation. She has added some shellfish, a little heat in the form of hot pepper flakes, and a marvelous orange-and-almond aïoli garnish.

¼ cup olive oil
4 cups finely diced yellow onions
3 large cloves garlic, minced
1 tablespoon red pepper flakes, or to taste
1 bay leaf
4 cups Fish Stock (see page 11)
1 cup fresh orange juice
¼ cup fresh lime or lemon juice
2 teaspoons grated orange zest
Salt and freshly ground black pepper to taste
60 Manila or other very small clams, well scrubbed
1½ pounds monkfish, cleaned and cut into 2-inch chunks
1 pound sea scallops, trimmed of tough side muscle
Orange-Almond Aïoli (recipe follows)

1 Assemble *mise en place* trays for this recipe (see page 7).

2 In a large sauté pan, heat the oil over medium heat. Add the onions and sauté for about 10 minutes, or until soft and translucent. Stir in the garlic, red pepper flakes, and bay leaf and sauté for 3 minutes. Add the stock and bring to a simmer. Reduce the heat and simmer for 15 minutes. Stir in the orange and lime juices, zest, and salt and pepper to taste.

3 Carefully drop the clams and fish chunks into the pan. Cover and simmer for about 5 minutes, or until the clams open. Carefully drop in the scallops and simmer for another 2 to 3 minutes, or until just cooked through and opaque.

4 Ladle into warm soup bowls. Place a dollop of the aïoli in the center of each bowl and serve immediately.

■ Flounder or rockfish can be substituted for the monkfish; add to the soup after the clams have cooked for 3 minutes.

■ You can garnish the soup with large croutons if desired.

■ Manilla clams are tiny clams, a little larger than a nickel. Substitute small cherrystones if necessary.

ORANGE-ALMOND AÏOLI
MAKES ABOUT 1½ CUPS

1 cup mayonnaise
¼ cup fresh orange juice
1 teaspoon fresh lemon juice
½ cup toasted sliced almonds, crushed
2 teaspoons puréed garlic
2 teaspoons grated orange zest
¼ teaspoon salt
Pinch of freshly ground black pepper

In a nonreactive bowl, whisk together the mayonnaise and orange and lemon juices. Whisk in the almonds, garlic, orange zest, and salt and pepper. Cover and refrigerate until ready to use.

NOTE: To prepare the crushed almonds, grind in a mortar and pestle or crush them with a rolling pin. To prepare the puréed garlic, process a few cloves in a mini food processor or grind in a mortar and pestle.

Spaghetti with Saffroned Onions, Greens, Fennel, Sun-Dried Tomatoes, and Currants

SERVES 6
PREPARATION TIME: ABOUT 30 MINUTES
COOKING TIME: ABOUT 15 MINUTES

This unusual pasta dish finds its roots in Sicily, with the Arabic influences of saffroned onions and currants combined with indigenous fennel and sun-dried tomatoes. It is complex in flavor and rich in taste, yet inexpensive and easy to prepare.

1 cup currants
1/4 teaspoon crushed saffron threads
2 tablespoons dry white wine
Coarse salt to taste
1 pound spaghetti
3/4 cup olive oil
4 onions, sliced 1/4 inch thick
2 cups 1/8-inch-thick fennel slices
3/4 to 1 cup finely julienned dry-packed sun-dried tomatoes (see Note)
2 tablespoons minced anchovy fillets
1 tablespoon minced garlic
1 1/2 pounds Swiss chard or escarole, trimmed, washed, dried, and cut into a fine chiffonade

1 Assemble *mise en place* trays for this recipe (see page 7).

2 In a small bowl, combine the currants and hot water to cover. Set aside to plump for at least 10 minutes. In a small cup, combine the saffron and wine. Set aside to soak.

3 Bring a large pot of salted water to a boil over high heat. Add the spaghetti and stir to prevent clumping. Cook for about 12 minutes, or until *al dente*.

4 Meanwhile, in a large sauté pan, heat the oil over medium heat. Add the onions and sauté for about 4 minutes, or until soft. Add the saffron mixture and cook for 1 minute. Stir in the fennel, sun-dried tomatoes, anchovies, and garlic and sauté for 3 minutes.

5 Drain the currants and add to the onion mixture. Stir in the Swiss chard and cook, stirring, for about 2 minutes, or until wilted.

6 Drain the pasta and transfer to a large shallow bowl. Add the sauce, toss to combine, and serve immediately on warm plates.

NOTE: Sun-dried tomatoes vary widely in quality and saltiness. If they are sweet, use the larger amount called for in the recipe; if salty, use the lesser.

Joyce says "no cheese, please" on this pasta. However, she says, you could add some chunks of grilled tuna for an even more flavorful and filling dish.

JOYCE GOLDSTEIN: *Spaghetti with Saffroned Onions, Greens, Fennel, Sun-Dried Tomatoes, and Currants*

Gateau Rolla

This rich dessert is a real crowd pleaser! And it is an even greater boon to the home cook as it is best made at least one day in advance.

MERINGUE LAYERS:
About 2 tablespoons flavorless vegetable oil
5 large egg whites, at room temperature
Pinch of salt
1 cup granulated sugar
1 teaspoon pure vanilla extract
¾ cup finely grated almonds

FILLING:
6 ounces sweet chocolate, coarsely chopped (see Note)
2 tablespoons nonalkalized cocoa powder
3 large egg whites
¾ cup granulated sugar
1½ cups (3 sticks) unsalted butter, at room temperature

1 Assemble *mise en place* trays for this recipe (see page 7).

2 Preheat the oven to 250 degrees F. Trace a circle 9 inches in diameter onto each of four 10-inch squares of parchment paper. Lightly oil 4 baking sheets with vegetable oil and place a piece of parchment paper onto each sheet, tracing side down. Lightly oil the paper. (See Note.)

3 To make the meringue layers, in a large bowl, using an electric mixer set on high speed, beat the egg whites with the salt until they hold stiff peaks. Gradually beat in ¾ cup of the sugar and continue to beat until stiff and glossy. Lower the speed and beat in the remaining ¼ cup sugar and the vanilla. Fold in the almonds just until blended.

4 Spread or pipe the meringue into rounds about ¼ inch thick on the parchment, staying within the outlines of the circles. Bake for about 1 hour, or until just dry. Carefully lift the meringues and paper off the baking sheets and cool on the paper on wire racks.

5 While the meringues are baking, make the filling: Melt the chocolate with the cocoa in the top half of a double boiler set over barely simmering water, stirring frequently until smooth. Set aside to cool.

6 Put the egg whites in a heatproof bowl and set it over a pan of hot water. Using an electric mixer set on high speed, beat until foamy. Gradually beat in the sugar until soft peaks form. Beat in the butter, a bit at a time, then beat in the chocolate mixture until smooth. Transfer to a clean bowl, cover, and refrigerate for about 1 hour, or until firm enough to spread.

7 Carefully peel the cooled meringue off the parchment paper. (If a meringue cracks or breaks, you can patch it with the filling.)

8 Spread equal portions of the chocolate filling over 3 of the meringue circles, spreading it about ¼ inch thick. Stack them on a cake plate. Place the remaining meringue on top and carefully frost the top and sides with the remaining chocolate filling.

9 Refrigerate the cake for about 1 hour, or until the frosting has set. Cover and allow to chill for at least 12 hours, or up to 2 days. Bring to room temperature before serving.

NOTE: This recipe calls for sweet chocolate, which is dark sweet chocolate, sweeter than bittersweet or semisweet chocolate. The most widely available brand in the United States is Baker's German Sweet Chocolate.

Only one 10-inch parchment paper square will fit on a baking sheet. You may have to bake these in two batches if your oven is not large enough to hold 4 baking sheets.

A NIGHT IN MOROCCO

*Ahi Tuna Tartare with Fennel, Caraway Toast,
and Green Olive Tapenade*

Lamb Tagine with Almonds, Dates, and Toasted Bulgur

Caramelized Pear and Cranberry Upside-Down Cake

WINE SUGGESTIONS:

Champagne or Sparkling Wine *(first course)*

Syrah (French, California, or Australian) *(second course)*

Tawny Port or Muscat de Beaumes-de-Venise *(dessert)*

WHAT YOU CAN PREPARE AHEAD OF TIME

Up to 1 week ahead: Make the Green Olive Tapenade. Cover and refrigerate. Prepare the Chicken Stock (if making your own).

Up to 2 days ahead: Make the Lamb Tagine with Almonds, Dates, and Toasted Bulgur, but omit the almonds and the final parsley addition. Cover and refrigerate. Reheat and garnish just before serving.

Early in the day: Make the Toasted Bulgur. Reheat as directed in the recipe note. Bake the Caramelized Pear and Cranberry Upside-Down Cake. Reheat as directed in the recipe note.

Up to 3 hours ahead: Prepare the Caraway Toasts for broiling.

Up to 1 hour ahead: Prepare the Ahi Tuna Tartare. Cover and refrigerate.

Up to 30 minutes ahead: Make the Fennel Salad.

Matthew Kenney is a New York chef who has been greatly influenced by the cuisines of the Mediterranean countries. He first came to my attention when he was chef at the very trendy Banana Cafe, but he became even more noticeable after he opened the stylish Matthew's Restaurant on Third Avenue in Manhattan. His food is well seasoned and full of flavor, with definite Mediterranean overtones. The menu that follows was a De Gustibus highlight, resulting after Chef Kenney attended an international food conference in Morocco. He returned enchanted with the foods that he had encountered and immediately began introducing them on his menu. His class benefited from his enthusiasms—we all caught the Moroccan magic and Matthew enthralled us with his gentle, earnest approach in the kitchen. The dishes are imaginative, light, and redolent with Moroccan influences.

◁ MATTHEW KENNEY: *Caramelized Pear and Cranberry Upside-Down Cake*

Ahi Tuna Tartare with Fennel, Caraway Toast, and Green Olive Tapenade

For this dish to be perfection, you must use sushi-grade tuna. If it is unavailable, substitute very fresh salmon. For a different take on this aromatic recipe, you could also marinate tuna fillets for about an hour in the tartare ingredients and then grill them.

3/4 pound very fresh sushi-grade tuna, cut into 1/8-inch dice
1 tablespoon plus 1 1/2 teaspoons grated lemon zest
1 tablespoon plus 1 1/2 teaspoons olive oil
1 1/2 teaspoons light soy sauce
1/4 cup plus 1 tablespoon minced fresh chives, flat-leaf parsley, or cilantro
Tabasco sauce to taste

Salt and freshly ground black pepper to taste
Fennel Salad (recipe follows)
Green Olive Tapenade (recipe follows)
Caraway Toast (recipe follows)
1/4 cup sliced pitted Picholine olives
2 tablespoons minced fresh fennel fronds (fennel tops)
Cracked black pepper to taste

1 Assemble *mise en place* trays for this recipe (see page 7).

2 In a medium-sized bowl, combine the tuna, lemon zest, oil, soy sauce, and chives. Toss gently. Add the Tabasco and salt and pepper to taste.

3 Place equal portions of the salad on 6 plates and spoon the tuna mixture on top. Spoon some tapenade around the edge and put a small amount on top of each portion of tuna. Arrange 4 toast quarters next to each salad and garnish the plates with the sliced olives and fennel fronds. Sprinkle with cracked pepper and serve.

■ To prevent sticking when cutting tuna (or other fish), rub the knife with a lightly oiled paper towel.

FENNEL SALAD
SERVES 6

2 medium-sized bulbs fennel, cut into small dice
1 tablespoon plus 1 1/2 teaspoons minced shallots
3/4 teaspoon freshly ground toasted coriander seeds
3 tablespoons fresh lemon juice
1 tablespoon plus 1 1/2 teaspoons sherry wine vinegar
1/2 to 2/3 cup walnut oil
Salt and freshly ground black pepper to taste

1 Put the fennel in a bowl.

2 In another bowl, combine the shallots, coriander, lemon juice, and vinegar. Whisk in the oil and season to taste with salt and pepper. Pour over the fennel and toss to combine. Serve immediately.

NOTE: Fennel quickly discolors, so it should not be cut more than 30 minutes before use. Although lemon juice inhibits discoloration, do not use more than called for in the dressing, as it would make the salad too acidic.

MATTHEW KENNEY: *Ahi Tuna Tartare with Fennel, Caraway Toast, and Green Olive Tapenade*

GREEN OLIVE TAPENADE
MAKES ABOUT ½ CUP

3 ounces Picholine olives, pitted (see page 9)
1½ teaspoons drained small capers
1½ anchovy fillets, patted dry
1½ teaspoons fresh lemon juice
¼ cup plus 2 tablespoons olive oil
About 2 tablespoons water
Salt and freshly ground black pepper to taste (optional)

1 In a blender, purée the olives, capers, and anchovies. Add the lemon juice and blend well. With the machine running, add the oil. Add enough water to make a thin sauce-like mixture. Season to taste with salt and pepper, if necessary.

2 Strain through a fine strainer into a bowl, pressing against the solids with the back of a spoon. Cover and refrigerate until ready to use.

CARAWAY TOASTS
MAKES 6 SLICES

2 tablespoons unsalted butter, at room temperature
1½ teaspoons freshly ground toasted caraway seeds
Pinch of salt
Six ¼-inch-thick slices slightly stale brioche, challah, or other egg-rich bread

1 Preheat the broiler.

2 Combine the butter, caraway, and salt. Spread on 1 side of each slice of brioche.

3 Toast under the broiler, butter side up, until lightly browned. Turn and toast the other side until lightly browned. Cut into quarters and serve warm.

NOTE: The bread can also be toasted on a charcoal or gas grill.

Lamb Tagine with Almonds, Dates, and Toasted Bulgur

SERVES 6
PREPARATION TIME: ABOUT 1 HOUR
COOKING TIME: ABOUT 2 HOURS

A tagine is a slowly simmered stew that is traditionally cooked in a wide earthenware dish with a conical lid (also called a tagine). This particular stew brings Morocco right into your kitchen by relying on the exotic dimension of sweet almonds, dates, and honey. It could also be served with couscous in place of bulgur.

¼ cup olive oil
1½ pounds boneless lamb shoulder, cut into 3/4-inch cubes
1 large onion, halved and sliced
1½ cups sliced carrots
¾ cup minced shallots
3 cloves garlic, minced
One 1-inch piece fresh ginger, peeled and minced
½ teaspoon saffron threads
1 tablespoon freshly ground toasted cumin seeds
1 tablespoon paprika
1 tablespoon ground cinnamon
1 teaspoon ground cardamom
¼ teaspoon ground allspice

About 3 cups Chicken Stock (see page 10)
¾ cup honey
¼ to ½ cup sliced pitted dates
Salt and freshly ground black pepper to taste
Cayenne pepper to taste
¼ cup plus 2 tablespoons chopped fresh flat-leaf parsley
Toasted Bulgur (recipe follows)
1 cup chopped toasted almonds

1 Assemble *mise en place* trays for this recipe (see page 7).

2 In a large Dutch oven, heat the oil over medium heat. Add the lamb and sear for about 5 minutes, or until well browned on all sides. Transfer to paper towels to drain.

3 Add the onions, carrots, shallots, garlic, and ginger to the Dutch oven and stir to combine. Add the saffron, cumin, paprika, cinnamon, cardamom, and allspice and cook, stirring occasionally, for about 10 minutes, or until the vegetables soften.

MATTHEW KENNEY: *Lamb Tagine with Almonds, Dates, and Toasted Bulgur*

4 Return the lamb to the Dutch oven, stir, and add just enough stock to barely cover the lamb. Reduce the heat, cover, and simmer gently for about 1 hour, or until the lamb is fork-tender and the liquid has reduced to a sauce-like consistency. Do not allow to boil.

5 Stir in the honey and ¼ cup dates. Taste for sweetness and add up to ¼ cup more dates if desired. Season to taste with salt and pepper and cayenne. Stir in ¼ cup of the parsley.

6 Mound the bulgur in the center of 6 plates. Spoon the tagine over the top and garnish with the almonds and the remaining 2 tablespoons parsley. Serve immediately.

NOTE: You can add chopped celery, potatoes, turnips, or other firm vegetables as well as diced prunes to the tagine.

TOASTED BULGUR
SERVES 6

1½ cups coarse-ground bulgur
3 tablespoons olive oil
1 large onion, chopped
¼ teaspoon hot green chile, such as jalapeño or serrano, seeded and chopped, or to taste
2 teaspoons tomato paste
1¾ cups plus 2 tablespoons boiling water
1 tablespoon plus 1½ teaspoons fresh lemon juice
¼ cup chopped fresh flat-leaf parsley
Salt and freshly ground black pepper to taste

1 Preheat the oven to 300 degrees F.

2 Spread the bulgur on a baking sheet and toast in the oven, stirring frequently, for about 7 minutes, or until light brown. Take care not to let bulgur get too dark, or it will taste burned. Set aside.

3 In a large skillet, heat the oil over medium heat. Add the onions and chile and sauté for about 4 minutes, or until the onions are soft and translucent. Stir in the bulgur and tomato paste, add the water, and bring to a boil. Stir gently, reduce the heat, cover, and cook for about 20 minutes, or until all the water has been absorbed and the bulgur is tender. Stir in the lemon juice, parsley, and salt and pepper to taste. Remove from the heat, cover, and let rest for 5 minutes before serving.

NOTE: If you prepare the bulgur early in the day, do so only up to the point of adding the lemon juice and parsley. To reheat, moisten with about ¼ cup Chicken Stock (see page 10) and warm over low heat. Add the lemon juice, parsley, and salt and pepper to taste just before serving. This may also be served at room temperature.

Caramelized Pear and Cranberry Upside-Down Cake

MAKES ONE 9-INCH CAKE; SERVES 6
PREPARATION TIME: ABOUT 20 MINUTES
COOKING TIME: ABOUT 5 MINUTES
BAKING TIME: ABOUT 30 MINUTES

Although this dessert is not Mediterranean in flavor, it is one of Matthew Kenney's trademarks and he wanted to share it with the class—and our readers.

11 tablespoons plus 1 teaspoon unsalted butter
¾ cup lightly packed light brown sugar
⅓ cup dried cranberries
2 firm but ripe pears, peeled, cored, halved, and sliced ⅛ inch thick
1⅔ cups all-purpose flour
2 teaspoons baking powder
¼ teaspoon salt
⅔ cup granulated sugar
2 large eggs
1 teaspoon pure vanilla extract
2 cups milk
Vanilla ice cream or frozen yogurt (optional)

■ Special Equipment: 9-inch round cake pan

1 Assemble *mise en place* trays for this recipe (see page 7).

2 Preheat the oven to 350 degrees F and put a baking sheet on the center rack. Lightly grease a 9-inch round cake pan.

3 In a medium-sized saucepan, melt 6 tablespoons of the butter over medium heat. Stir in the brown sugar and cook, stirring constantly, for about 5 minutes, or until the sugar dissolves. Immediately pour into the prepared cake pan. Sprinkle the cranberries over the sugar syrup and arrange the pear slices on top in a slightly overlapping circular pattern. Set aside.

4 In a small bowl, whisk together the flour, baking powder, and salt.

5 In a large bowl, using an electric mixer set on medium-high speed, cream the remaining ⅓ cup butter and the granulated sugar for 2 to 3 minutes, or until light and fluffy. Add the eggs 1 at a time, and beat until well combined. Add the vanilla. Add the dry ingredients, alternating them with the milk and beating until well blended. Pour the batter over the pears and spread with a spatula to cover the fruit.

6 Set the cake on the preheated baking sheet and bake for about 30 minutes, or until the edges are golden and a cake tester inserted in the center comes out clean. Cool on a wire rack for 5 minutes.

7 Position a serving plate over the cake pan and gently invert. Tap gently to release, and lift the pan off the cake. Serve warm, with scoops of ice cream or yogurt if desired.

NOTE: The dessert pictured was prepared as individual 6-inch cakes. If you chose to bake individual cakes, divide the pears and batter among the smaller cake pans and decrease the baking time to about 20 minutes, or until the edges are golden and a cake tester inserted in the center comes out clean.

Baking the cake on the hot baking sheet helps to caramelize the sugar. If making the cake in advance, invert it onto an oven-proof plate. Just before serving, reheat it in a 300-degree-F oven for about 10 minutes.

A Robust Winter Dinner

Baked Cod with Bulgur

Braised Lamb Shanks with White Bean Purée

Pistachio-Fig Tart

Wine Suggestions:

Sauvignon Blanc or Chardonnay *(first course)*

Merlot or Pinot Noir *(second course)*

Tawny Port *(dessert)*

What You Can Prepare Ahead of Time

Up to 1 week ahead: Prepare the Veal Stock and Chicken Stock (if making your own).

Up to 3 days ahead: Prepare the Braised Lamb Shanks up to point of straining off the liquid. Cover and refrigerate. Reheat as directed in the recipe note. Prepare the White Bean Purée. Cover and refrigerate. Reheat as directed in the recipe note.

Up to 1 day ahead: Make the Pistachio-Fig Tart.

Early in the day: Prepare the vegetables for the Baked Cod with Bulgur, cover, and refrigerate.

Whenever Tom Valenti teaches at De Gustibus, we know we are in for a special evening. Not only is his food always scrumptious and easy to prepare, his sense of humor keeps the kitchen rocking. Plus, he manages to make everything look almost effortless—a wonderful combination of qualities in a chef.

I first met Tom when he was working at New York's Gotham Bar and Grill and arrived at De Gustibus as assistant to Chef Alfred Portale. Chef Valenti later moved on to much acclaim at the warm and friendly Alison on Dominick. In the spring of 1994, he became chef and co-owner at Cascabel, where he delights diners with his unique blend of French and Italian cooking. The recipes he shares with us here are some of our all-time favorites and represent but a few of Tom's signature dishes.

◁ TOM VALENTI: *Braised Lamb Shanks with White Bean Purée*

Baked Cod with Bulgur

Cod is not often on the De Gustibus menu, but after tasting Tom's version, we decided it should be a regular item. Although he served it as a first course, I think it makes a terrific, easy-to-put-together entrée.

15 Sicilian or other large green olives, pitted and sliced
9 shallots, thinly sliced
3 tomatoes, cored, seeded, and chopped
3 cloves garlic, sliced
1 lemon, peeled and sectioned
1 teaspoon minced fresh tarragon
1 teaspoon minced fresh oregano
¾ cup dry white wine
½ cup water
Salt and freshly ground black pepper to taste
Six 6-ounce pieces skinless cod fillet
1½ cups bulgur
2½ cups plus 2 tablespoons boiling salted water
¾ cup extra-virgin olive oil

1 Assemble *mise en place* trays for this recipe (see page 7).

2 Preheat the oven to 450 degrees F. Lightly oil a baking dish large enough to hold the fish easily.

3 In a medium-sized bowl, combine the olives, shallots, tomatoes, garlic, lemon, tarragon, oregano, wine, water, and salt and pepper to taste. Pour into the baking dish and lay the fish on top. Cover tightly with aluminum foil. Reduce the oven temperature to 400 degrees F and bake for about 15 minutes, or until the fish is firm to the touch. Set aside uncovered to cool slightly.

4 Meanwhile, put the bulgur in a heat-proof bowl. Add the boiling water, cover tightly with plastic wrap, and set aside for about 15 minutes, or until all the water has been absorbed.

5 Carefully pour the cooking liquid from the baking pan into a blender and process until smooth. With the motor running, slowly add the oil, blending until the mixture is emulsified and smooth.

6 Spoon an equal portion of bulgur onto each plate. Place a fish fillet on top, arrange the vegetables on top of the fish and the bulgur, and drizzle with the sauce. Serve immediately.

TOM VALENTI: *Baked Cod with Bulgur*

Braised Lamb Shanks with White Bean Purée

SERVES 6
PREPARATION TIME: ABOUT 30 MINUTES
SOAKING TIME (BEANS ONLY): 8 HOURS
COOKING TIME: ABOUT 2 HOURS AND 40 MINUTES

This is Chef Tom Valenti's best-known signature dish and I guarantee it deserves its starring role on his menu. It is a terrific do-ahead winter meal!

6 lamb shanks
Salt and freshly ground black pepper to taste
1/2 cup olive oil
8 ribs celery, sliced
2 large carrots, sliced
1 large onion, diced
5 cloves garlic, minced
2 cups red wine
2 cups Veal Stock (see page 10)
Two 32-ounce cans Italian plum tomatoes, drained and crushed
6 anchovy fillets
20 black or green peppercorns
2 bay leaves
White Bean Purée (recipe follows)

1 Assemble *mise en place* trays for this recipe (see page 7).

2 Preheat the oven to 325 degrees F.

3 Season the shanks with salt and pepper to taste. In a large sauté pan, heat the olive oil over medium heat. Add the shanks and sear for about 6 minutes, or until browned on all sides. Transfer to a large flame-proof casserole or roasting pan.

4 In the same pan, sauté the celery, carrots, onions, and garlic over medium heat for 30 seconds, taking care not to burn any particles that have stuck to the bottom of the pan. Add 1 cup of the wine and stir to deglaze the pan. Scrape the mixture over the shanks.

5 Add the veal stock, the remaining 1 cup wine, the tomatoes, anchovies, peppercorns and bay leaves to the casserole. The shanks should be almost covered with liquid; if necessary, add some water. Stir to combine. Bring to a boil over medium-high heat, remove from the heat, and cover tightly.

6 Bake for 2 1/2 hours, or until the meat is almost falling off the bone. Using tongs or a slotted spoon, remove the shanks and set aside, covered with aluminum foil to keep warm. Strain the cooking liquid through a fine sieve into a medium-sized saucepan and simmer for about 5 minutes over medium heat, or until reduced and thickened slightly.

7 Place an equal portion of bean purée on each plate. Place a shank alongside and spoon some sauce over the top. Pass the remaining sauce on the side.

NOTE: You can prepare the shanks ahead of time, up to the point of straining off the liquid. Reheat them in a 350-degree-F oven for about 20 minutes and complete the recipe as instructed.

WHITE BEAN PURÉE

SERVES 6

1 pound dried Great Northern beans
4 cloves garlic, 3 crushed and 1 minced
4 sprigs fresh thyme
2 bay leaves
3 cups Chicken Stock (see page 10), or more if needed
1/2 cup white wine
Salt and freshly ground black pepper to taste
1/2 cup olive oil
1 to 2 tablespoons unsalted butter, at room temperature (optional)

1 Rinse the beans in cold water, discarding any damaged or broken ones. Place in a large bowl, add cold water to cover, and soak for 8 hours, changing the water 3 or 4 times. Drain.

2 In a large saucepan, combine the beans, crushed garlic, thyme, bay leaves, stock, and wine and bring to a simmer over medium heat. Cook for about 1 1/2 hours, or until the beans are tender, adding additional stock or water if the beans get too dry. Season to taste with salt and pepper.

3 In a food processor fitted with the metal blade, purée the beans. With the motor running, slowly add the olive oil and minced garlic and process until smooth. (This may have to be done in batches.) If the purée seems too thick, fold in the butter. Serve hot.

NOTE: You can prepare the beans ahead of time. Reheat over low heat, adding extra stock or water if necessary.

Pistachio-Fig Tart

Tom told us that, as a boy, he adored Fig Newtons. When he learned to cook, one of his goals was to make a "grown-up" version of his childhood favorite. This is his delicious tribute to the famous cookie, devised with Paula Smith, the original pastry chef at Alison on Dominick.

FILLING:

1¼ pounds dried figs, stems removed
1½ cups granulated sugar
3 tablespoons ground cinnamon
1 tablespoon ground cloves
½ teaspoon ground mace
Pinch of salt
1 teaspoon freshly ground black pepper
1½ cups water
1 cup white wine

PASTRY:

1½ cups plus 3 tablespoons all-purpose flour
1 cup granulated sugar
1 cup finely ground pistachios
2 teaspoons baking powder
Grated zest of 1 lemon
1 cup (2 sticks) plus 2 tablespoons unsalted butter, at room temperature
3 large eggs
1 large egg yolk
1 teaspoon pure vanilla extract
2 tablespoons milk

■ Special Equipment: 10-inch tart pan with removable bottom; pastry bag fitted with No. 5 plain tip

1 Assemble *mise en place* trays for this recipe (see page 7).

2 To make the filling, in a large nonreactive saucepan, combine the figs, sugar, cinnamon, cloves, mace, salt, pepper, water, and wine and bring to a boil over medium-high heat. Reduce the heat and simmer for about 30 minutes, or until the figs are tender and the liquid has reduced to a thick syrup. Set aside to cool to room temperature.

3 In a food processor fitted with the metal blade, purée the figs with their liquid. Transfer to a bowl and set aside.

4 Preheat the oven to 350 degrees F. Lightly oil a 10-inch tart pan with a removable bottom.

5 To make the pastry, in a large bowl, combine the flour, sugar, pistachios, baking powder, and lemon zest. Add the butter and, using an electric mixer set on low speed, mix until blended. Add 2 of the eggs, the egg yolk, and vanilla and beat on medium speed until combined.

6 Spread half the dough in the bottom of the prepared tart pan. Top with the fig mixture, leaving a 1-inch border all around.

7 Place the remaining dough in a pastry bag fitted with a No. 5 plain tip. Pipe a lattice design on top of the tart, allowing the ends to fall over the edges of the pan. Fold the ends under themselves and pat into place so they adhere to the bottom crust.

8 In a small bowl, whisk together the milk and the remaining egg. Using a pastry brush, coat the lattice with the egg wash. Bake for about 30 minutes, or until the pastry is golden brown. Cool on a wire rack for about 10 minutes, cut into wedges, and serve warm.

◁ TOM VALENTI: *Pistachio-Fig Tart*

A WORLD OF FOOD

Hot and Sweet Red Pepper Dip with Walnuts and Pomegranate
MUHAMMARA

Flaked Parsley Salad with Black Olives

Couscous with Greens

Sweet and Sour Pumpkin or Butternut Squash

Mussels "Saganaki"

Walnut Roll

WINE SUGGESTIONS:

Dry Spanish Wine or Dry Rosé *(red pepper dip)*

Gavi or Pinot Grigio *(parsley salald, couscous, and squash)*

Sauvignon Blanc *(mussels)*

Tawny Port *(dessert)*

WHAT YOU CAN PREPARE AHEAD OF TIME

Up to 1 week ahead: Make and freeze the Walnut Roll. Thaw in the refrigerator before serving. Make the Hot and Sweet Red Pepper Dip.

Up to 2 days ahead: Prepare the Sweet and Sour Pumpkin or Butternut Squash.

Early in the day: Prepare the parsley for the Flaked Parsley Salad. Wrap in damp paper towels and refrigerate. Steam the greens for the Couscous with Greens. Cover and refrigerate. Prepare the Mussels "Saganaki" up to the addition of the feta. Before serving, soak the feta and proceed as directed in the recipe through step 5.

Paula Wolfert was one of the original teachers at De Gustibus more than fifteen years ago. She was, in fact, one of the first cooks to bring the foods of the Mediterranean to the classroom—it was she who introduced us to the then-unfamiliar preserved lemons, which now are almost commonplace. Paula brought so much passion, romance, and history to the stove that we were all entranced. She has returned many times to tell us tales of her culinary adventures as she roams the Mediterranean countries looking for traditional recipes to bring back to the home cook.

◁ PAULA WOLFERT: *Couscous with Greens, Mussels "Saganaki,"* and *Sweet and Sour Pumpkin*

Hot and Sweet Red Pepper Dip with Walnuts and Pomegranate

MAKES ABOUT 3 CUPS
PREPARATION TIME: ABOUT 15 MINUTES
CHILLING TIME: AT LEAST 8 HOURS

Muhammara

This is a very tasty dip that, if covered and refrigerated, will last for at least a week. Serve with crisp bread, crackers, or pita triangles.

6 to 8 red bell peppers (about 2½ pounds), roasted, peeled, and seeds and membranes removed
1½ cups coarsely ground walnuts (about 6 ounces)
½ cup crumbled unsalted crackers
2 tablespoons pomegranate molasses
1 tablespoon fresh lemon juice
½ teaspoon ground cumin, plus a pinch
½ teaspoon granulated sugar
¾ teaspoon salt
3 tablespoons olive oil
2 small hot chiles, such as Fresno or hot Hungarian, roasted, peeled, and seeds and membranes removed, or to taste
2 tablespoons toasted pine nuts

PAULA WOLFERT: *Hot and Sweet Red Pepper Dip with Walnuts and Pomegranate* and *Flaked Parsley Salad with Black Olives*

1 Assemble *mise en place* trays for this recipe (see page 7).

2 Spread the bell peppers, smooth side up, on paper towels and drain for about 10 minutes.

3 In a food processor fitted with the metal blade, combine the walnuts, crackers, pomegranate molasses, lemon juice, ½ teaspoon of the cumin, the sugar, and salt and process until smooth. Add the bell peppers and process until puréed and creamy. With the motor running, add 2 table-spoons of the oil in a thin stream. Add the chiles. If the dip seems too thick, thin it with 1 to 2 tablespoons water. Transfer to a nonreactive container, cover, and refrigerate for at least 8 hours.

4 Place the dip in a serving dish and sprinkle with the pine nuts and the pinch of cumin. Drizzle with the remaining 1 tablespoon oil.

Flaked Parsley Salad with Black Olives

SERVES 6
PREPARATION TIME: ABOUT 25 MINUTES

This unusual recipe uses everyday curly parsley and is delicious with fish. Do not mix this ahead of time.

¼ pound (about 2 large bunches) very fresh curly parsley, washed and thoroughly dried
24 Kalamata or Niçoise olives, rinsed, drained, pitted, and slivered
3 tablespoons minced shallots
½ teaspoon Worcestershire sauce
3 tablespoons olive oil
1 tablespoon cider vinegar or rice wine vinegar
Salt and freshly ground black pepper to taste
3 tablespoons freshly grated Pecorino-Romano cheese

1 Assemble *mise en place* trays for this recipe (see page 7).

2 Remove the parsley leaves from the stems, discarding the stems, and tear each leaf into tiny bits. You should have about 4 loosely packed cups of parsley flakes.

3 In a large bowl, combine the parsley, olives, shallots, Worcestershire, oil, vinegar, and salt and pepper to taste and toss gently. Transfer to a serving bowl and sprinkle with the cheese. Serve immediately.

NOTE: To insure the parsley is completely dry use a salad spinner.

Couscous with Greens

This is a delicious, nutritious entrée for vegetarians and those looking for healthy alternatives in their diets.

½ pound (about 4 bunches) fresh flat-leaf parsley, thick stems discarded, and chopped
¼ pound (about 2 bunches) fresh dill, chopped
¼ pound fennel fronds (fennel tops), chopped
¼ pound (about 2 bunches) scallions, chopped
¼ pound leeks, chopped
½ cup chopped carrot greens or celery leaves (optional)
½ cup olive oil
1 cup chopped onions
3 tablespoons tomato paste
2 tablespoons crushed garlic, plus 6 whole garlic cloves, peeled
2 teaspoons sweet paprika
2 teaspoons ground coriander or tabil
1 teaspoon ground caraway seeds
2 teaspoons salt, or more to taste
1½ to 2 teaspoons red pepper flakes, preferably Aleppo, Turkish, or Near East
2 cups hot water
1 pound (about 2½ cups) medium-grain couscous
1 red bell pepper, cored, seeded, and cut into 6 pieces
1 hot green chile, seeded and minced

■ Special Equipment: Couscous cooker (couscousière), or a large steamer or a large colander that fits inside a large saucepan

1 Assemble *mise en place* trays for this recipe (see page 7).

2 In the perforated top of a *couscousière* (or a steamer basket or large colander), combine the parsley, dill, fennel, scallions, leeks, and carrot greens or celery leaves, if using, and set over boiling water. Cover and steam for 30 minutes. Remove from the heat, uncover, and let stand until cool enough to handle. Squeeze out the excess moisture and set aside.

3 In a large sauté pan, heat the oil over medium heat. Add the onions and sauté for 3 minutes, or until tender. Stir in the tomato paste and cook, stirring constantly, for about 2 minutes, or until the paste glistens. Stir in the crushed garlic, paprika, coriander, caraway, salt, and red pepper flakes. Reduce the heat and sauté for about 3 minutes, or until the garlic softens. Add 1 cup of the water, cover, and cook for 15 minutes.

4 Remove from the heat, add the couscous, and stir until well combined. Add the steamed vegetables and herbs and stir to combine. Fold in the bell pepper, chile, and garlic cloves.

5 Fill the bottom of the *couscousière* with water and bring to a boil over high heat. Fasten on the perforated top and put the couscous mixture in the top. (Or put it into the steamer basket or large colander and set over boiling water.) Cover and steam for 30 minutes.

6 Transfer the couscous to a warm serving dish and break up any lumps with a fork. Remove and reserve the garlic cloves and bell pepper. Stir the remaining cup of hot water into the couscous, taste, and adjust the seasoning. Cover with aluminum foil and let stand for 10 minutes. Remove the foil and garnish the couscous with the reserved bell pepper and garlic.

PAULA WOLFERT: *Couscous with Greens*

Sweet and Sour Pumpkin or Butternut Squash

SERVES 6
PREPARATION TIME: ABOUT 15 MINUTES
COOKING TIME: ABOUT 15 MINUTES
RESTING TIME (LIQUID): 3 TO 4 HOURS

This is an interesting way of preparing squash. It serves as either a condiment or a side dish.

One 2 1/2-pound pumpkin or butternut squash
About 2 tablespoons coarse salt
1/4 cup olive oil
1 1/3 cups (about 1/2 pound) thinly sliced onions
1 teaspoon granulated sugar
1/4 cup plus 3 tablespoons white wine vinegar
1/3 cup water
3/4 teaspoon salt
1/2 teaspoon freshly ground black pepper
1/4 cup torn fresh mint leaves

1 Assemble *mise en place* trays for this recipe (see page 7).

2 Peel the pumpkin or squash, removing a little flesh with the peel. If using pumpkin, cut the flesh into 1/4-inch-thick slices approximately 2 1/2 inches by 3 1/4 inches. If using butternut squash, start at the neck end and cut into 1/4-inch-thick rounds. When you reach the bulb end, cut lengthwise in half, remove the seeds and pulp, and slice the flesh into 1-inch squares about 1/4 inch thick. Sprinkle the pumpkin or squash lightly with coarse salt. Using paper towels, blot off the excess moisture, but do not dry completely.

3 In a large nonreactive skillet, heat the oil over medium-high heat. Add the pumpkin or squash, without crowding, and cook for about 5 minutes, turning once or twice, or until golden brown on both sides. Remove with tongs and drain on paper towels, then cover and set aside.

4 Reduce the heat to medium and add the onions and sugar to the skillet. Cook for about 5 minutes, or until the onions are soft and golden brown and just beginning to caramelize. Raise the heat, add the vinegar and water, and bring to a simmer. Cook for about 4 minutes, or until the liquid has reduced by half. Remove from the heat and set aside to mellow for 3 to 4 hours.

5 Layer the pumpkin or squash on a large serving dish, sprinkling the layers with the salt and pepper. Pour the onion mixture over the slices. Garnish with half the torn mint leaves, cover, and refrigerate for about 1 hour, or until chilled.

6 Serve chilled, garnished with the remaining mint leaves.

NOTE: For the sweetest flesh, purchase pumpkin or squash with dull skin that feels heavy for its size. It is essential to use a mild wine vinegar for this recipe. Try the Sasso brand or French Corcellet white wine vinegar for best results. Avoid vinegar with more than 6 percent acidity.

◁ PAULA WOLFERT:
Sweet and Sour Pumpkin

PAULA WOLFERT:
Mussels "Saganaki" ▷

Mussels "Saganaki"

A saganaki is a shallow pan with two handles, but any deep sauté pan will work just about as well for this combination of shellfish and feta cheese. The flavors may surprise your taste buds, but I'm sure you will find it quite delicious.

3 pounds mussels
1 tablespoon coarse salt, plus more to taste
1/2 cup water
1 to 2 tablespoons fresh lemon juice, or more to taste
1/4 teaspoon freshly ground black pepper, plus more to taste
1 tablespoon olive oil

2 teaspoons minced seeded long hot green chile, or more to taste
1/3 cup plus 2 tablespoons chopped fresh flat-leaf parsley
1/2 cup peeled, seeded, and chopped fresh tomatoes or drained, seeded, and chopped canned tomatoes
1/2 teaspoon mashed garlic
5 large fresh spearmint or other mint leaves, torn into shreds
1/4 teaspoon crumbled dried oregano, preferably Greek
1 teaspoon dry mustard
Pinch of red pepper flakes
3 ounces imported feta cheese, preferably Bulgarian

1 Assemble *mise en place* trays for this recipe (see page 7).

2 Scrub the mussels and pull off the beards. Rinse in several changes of water and put in a bowl of cool water. Add the sea salt and let stand for at least 30 minutes to purge the mussels of sand. Drain.

3 Place the mussels in a saganaki or large deep sauté pan. Add the water, cover, and cook over high heat for about 2 minutes, or just until the mussels open; do not overcook. Using tongs or a slotted spoon, transfer the mussels to a bowl to cool. Strain the cooking liquid through several layers of damp cheesecloth into a bowl and set aside.

4 Remove the mussels from their shells and cut off any remaining beards. Strain any liquid collected in the bowl and add to the reserved mussel broth. Sprinkle the mussels with lemon juice and pepper to taste.

5 In a medium-sized nonreactive skillet, heat the olive oil over medium-low heat. Add 2 teaspoons minced chile and 1/3 cup of the parsley and cook for 1 minute, stirring. Add the reserved mussel cooking liquid, the tomatoes, garlic,

mint, oregano, mustard, red pepper flakes, and the remaining 1/4 teaspoon pepper. Raise the heat to high and bring to a boil. Reduce the heat and simmer for 5 minutes, stirring often, or until the sauce has reduced to about 1 1/4 cups. If desired, add more minced green chile to taste. Return to the boil for just a second. Transfer to a bowl and allow to cool for about 10 minutes, until tepid. Add the mussels to the sauce, cover, and refrigerate.

6 Twenty minutes before serving, soak the feta in cold water for 15 minutes. Drain and cut into 1/2-inch cubes.

7 In a large skillet, heat the mussels and sauce over medium-low heat just until heated through. Do not allow the sauce to boil. Add the feta cheese and cook, stirring, for 2 minutes. Taste and adjust the seasoning. Serve immediately, sprinkled with the remaining 2 tablespoons chopped parsley.

■ If you buy cultivated, farm-raised mussels, there is no need to soak them. Ask the fish merchant where the mussels come from; soaking diminishes their flavor.

Walnut Roll

MAKES ONE 17-INCH ROLL; SERVES 6 TO 8
PREPARATION TIME: ABOUT 30 MINUTES
BAKING TIME: ABOUT 15 MINUTES
CHILLING TIME: AT LEAST 2 HOURS

This dessert is rich enough to end any meal in grand style.

CAKE:

2 tablespoons unsalted butter, at room temperature
5 large eggs, separated
1/2 cup granulated sugar
Pinch of salt
1 1/4 cups finely ground walnuts (about 5 ounces)
1/2 teaspoon baking powder

FILLING:

1 1/2 cups ground walnuts (about 6 ounces)
1/2 cup hot milk
8 tablespoons unsalted butter, at room temperature
1/3 cup granulated sugar
2 tablespoons Cognac
1 cup heavy cream, whipped to soft peaks
About 1/2 cup confectioners' sugar

■ Special Equipment: 11 x 17-inch jelly roll pan

1 Assemble *mise en place* trays for this recipe (see page 7).

2 Preheat the oven to 375 degrees F. Using 1 tablespoon of the butter, grease an 11 x 17-inch jelly-roll pan. Line the pan with wax or parchment paper, leaving a 2-inch overhang at each end, and press down on the butter. Using the remaining 1 tablespoon butter, grease the paper.

3 To make the cake, in a large bowl, using an electric mixer set on medium-high speed, beat the egg yolks until foamy. Beat in the sugar and salt until pale and thick. Using a large wire whisk, fold in the nuts and baking powder.

4 In another large bowl, using the mixer set on medium-high speed, beat the egg whites until they hold stiff peaks. Using a spatula, fold the egg whites into the yolk mixture. Spread evenly in the prepared pan.

5 Bake for 15 minutes, or until a cake tester inserted in the center comes out clean. Cool slightly on a rack, cover with a damp kitchen cloth, and refrigerate for 30 minutes.

PAULA WOLFERT: *Walnut Roll*

6 To prepare the filling, put the walnuts in a bowl and pour the milk over them. Allow to cool.

7 In a large bowl, using an electric mixer set on medium-high speed, cream the butter. Gradually add the sugar and beat until light and fluffy. Beat in the nut mixture and the Cognac. Using a spatula, fold in the whipped cream.

8 Sprinkle the cake with confectioners' sugar. Lay a 20-inch-long sheet of wax paper over the cake. Grip the ends of the jelly-roll pan, holding the wax paper firmly in place, and quickly invert the cake and pan onto a work surface. Remove the pan and peel the paper from the cake. Using a spatula, spread the filling over the cake. Using the second sheet of wax paper to help guide it, roll up the cake like a jelly roll. Cover with foil and refrigerate for at least 1½ hours, or until the filling is set. Just before serving, dust the top of the cake with confectioners' sugar.

NOTE: Use a nut grinder to grind the nuts fine for the cake and the grating blade of a food processor to grind them less fine for the filling.

Glossary

Aïoli: A pungent garlic-flavored mayonnaise commonly used in the Provence region of France.

Al dente: Italian term meaning, literally, "to the tooth." Most often used to describe pasta that has been cooked until it is just tender but still offers some resistance when chewed. Can also be used to describe the degree to which certain vegetables should be cooked.

Ancho chile powder: A dark brown, mildly hot, sweet pure chile powder made from ground ancho chiles, or *chiles negros*. Available in Hispanic and other special markets.

Arborio rice: Medium-grain, plump, high-starch rice used in Italian cooking, most often to make the traditional risotto. The best is imported from Italy.

Balsamic vinegar: Italian specialty vinegar that has been produced in Modena for centuries. It is made from the boiled-down must of white grapes. True balsamic vinegar is aged for decades in a succession of different types of wood barrels.

Bouquet garni: A combination of herbs tied together or wrapped in a cheesecloth bag and used to flavor sauces, stews, soups, and stocks. The classic French combination is parsley, thyme, and bay leaf.

Bulgur wheat: Steamed, dried, and crushed wheat berries, used extensively in Middle Eastern cooking. Available in coarse, medium, and fine grinds.

Butterfly: To split any ingredient, such as shrimp or meat, in half down the center without cutting completely through it. The two halves are opened to form a butterfly shape.

Cappuccino: Italian coffee made by topping espresso with hot, frothy, steamed milk. Ground cinnamon or cocoa may be sprinkled on top.

Chiffonade: A preparation of greens, classically sorrel, chicory, or lettuce, cut into strips of varying degrees of thickness, easily done by rolling the leaves up cigar-fashion and slicing crosswise. Used as a garnish for soups and cold hors d'oeuvres.

Cilantro: Pungent herb that looks like flat-leaf parsley, used to flavor Asian, Indian, Latin American, and other dishes. The bright green leaves are sometimes referred to as Chinese parsley or fresh coriander. Cilantro is widely available. There is no substitute. Do not use coriander seeds instead!

Clarified butter: Butter that has been heated and skimmed so that all the milk solids are removed, leaving only the clear yellow fat. See page 9 for instructions for clarifying butter.

Couscous: Granular semolina that is a staple of North Africa, particularly Morocco. The term also refers to a dish for which a meat and/or vegetable stew is cooked in the bottom of a *couscousiere* (the special pot used only for this dish) while the couscous it will top steams in the perforated upper half.

Fava beans: Pale, tannish-green, flat pod beans with a tough outer skin that must be removed, usually by blanching, before eating. Used frequently in Mediterranean and Middle Eastern cuisines.

Fennel: A licorice-scented plant having a bulbous base, celery-like ribs, and feathery foliage. Used extensively in Mediterranean cooking for its sweetly aromatic anise flavor.

Feta cheese: A tangy Greek, Bulgarian or Israeli sheep or goat's milk cheese that is cured in a salty brine.

Fresno chile: Fairly mild, triangular-shaped chile that usually is marketed green, although it can be yellow or red when mature.

Gorgonzola cheese: Rich, creamy, blue-veined Italian cow's milk cheese with a strong, musty flavor. Best used as soon as it has been cut from a wheel, since it quickly loses moisture. Named for the town where it was first produced.

Guacamole: Mexican dip or sauce made from mashed avocado flavored with chiles and citrus juice. Tomato, cilantro, garlic, and scallions are frequent additions.

Hand-held immersion blender: A long, portable blender with a blade at the bottom that can be put directly into a saucepan or deep pot to purée sauces, soups, and other mixtures.

Harissa: An extremely hot Tunisian sauce made from chiles, garlic, and spices. Used to flavor stews and soups and, most particularly, as an accompaniment to couscous.

Israeli couscous: A toasted wheat pasta larger and softer than traditional couscous. Available at specialty stores.

Jalapeño: Small, triangular-shaped, hot green chile. Can be bright red when mature, Jalapeños are often sold pickled.

Julienne: Refers to ingredients, particularly vegetables, that have been cut into uniform thin strips, usually about the size of a matchstick. The vegetable to be julienned is first cut into slices of uniform thickness and then the slices are stacked and cut into even strips. Classically, these strips are 1 to 2 inches long by ¼ inch thick. Usually used as a decorative garnish. See page 9 for instructions for preparing julienne.

Kalamata olive: A large purple-black Greek olive cured in a wine vinegar brine. May be packed in oil or vinegar.

Manchego cheese: A mellow, semi-firm Spanish sheep's milk cheese, originally made only with milk from Manchego sheep. Available at fine cheese shops and Spanish markets.

Mince: To chop very fine.

Mortar: A round, concave container, usually made of marble, porcelain, or wood, used to hold foods that are to be hand-ground using a pestle.

Niçoise olive: Very small brownish-black brine-cured French olive often packed in olive oil, and, frequently, herbs.

Parmigiano-Reggiano cheese: Grainy, hard, dry, pale amber Italian part-skimmed cow's milk cheese with a sharp-sweet taste. Parmigiano-Reggiano is the most eminent of all Parmesan cheeses; its name is always stamped on the rind of cheeses produced in the areas surrounding the Parma and Reggio Emilia regions.

Pestle: A utensil used to pound food in a mortar. It can be rounded or pointed depending on the mortar. It is usually made of the same material as the mortar.

Phyllo (also filo): Tissue-paper–thin Greek pastry dough, usually buttered and stacked in layers to enclose sweet or savory mixtures. Available in most supermarkets.

Picholine olive: Long, pointy, pale green brine-cured Provençal olive packed in vinegar or, at times, olive oil.

Poussin: French term for a very young, small chicken weighing about one to one and a half pounds. Also called squab chicken.

Prosciutto: Italian salt-cured and air-dried ham that has been slow-aged for a dense texture and delicate, sweet flavor. Italy's Parma ham is the traditional prosciutto.

Ramp: A wild leek that grows in the spring all along the Eastern seaboard and has a strong onion flavor with hints of garlic. Scallions or leeks are sometimes used in place of ramps but lack their distinctive flavor.

Risotto: A rich, creamy Italian rice dish created by gradually stirring a liquid into medium-grained rice (such as Arborio) that has been sautéed in oil and aromatics.

Saffron: An intensely aromatic spice from the dried stigmas of a small crocus. It is the world's most costly spice, as it takes about 70,000 stigmas to make one pound. It is an integral part of many Mediterranean dishes, imparting a yellow-orange color and a somewhat bitter flavor to paella, bouillabaisse, and risotto Milanese, among other foods.

Sear: To brown meat or poultry by cooking over (or under) intense heat. This process is used to seal in the juices before longer cooking.

Sumac: A reddish-brown, salty-sour powder ground from the berries of one variety of sumac plant. Used extensively in Middle Eastern cooking.

Tabil: A Tunisian seasoning made by pounding garlic, red bell peppers, chile peppers, cilantro, and caraway seeds together. Used to enhance the flavors of soups and stews.

Tahini: A thick paste made from ground sesame seeds. Used extensively in Middle Eastern cooking.

Tapenade: A Provençal condiment made from olives, capers, and anchovies seasoned with garlic, olive oil, and, sometimes, herbs.

Tarama: Carp or mullet roe, used extensively in Greek cooking. Usually available canned.

Tartare: Coarsely chopped raw meat or fish, seasoned with herbs, salt, and pepper and served uncooked.

Temper: To introduce a small amount of hot liquid into a cold mixture before it is added to a larger amount of hot liquid, to keep the cold mixture from curdling as it is incorporated into the hot. Tempering is a technique often used with egg preparations.

Sources

Dean & Deluca
560 Broadway
New York, NY 10012
1-800-221-7714
212-431-1691

Katagiri & Company, Inc.
224 East 59th Street
New York, NY 10022
212-755-3566

Balducci's
424 Avenue of the Americas
New York, NY 10011
212-673-2600

Balducci's Mail Order Division
1102 Queens Plaza South
Long Island City, NY 11101
1-800-BALDUCCI

Kalustyan Orient Export Trading Corporation
(Middle Eastern and Indian ingredients)
123 Lexington Avenue
New York, NY 10016
212-685-3451

Sahadi Importing Companies
(Middle Eastern and Indian ingredients)
187-89 Atlantic Avenue
Brooklyn, NY 11201
718-624-4550

Index

CONVERSION CHART

WEIGHTS AND MEASURES

1 teaspoon = 5 milliliters

1 tablespoon = 3 teaspoons = 15 milliliters

$1/8$ cup = 2 tablespoons = 1 fluid ounce = 30 milliliters

$1/4$ cup = 4 tablespoons = 2 fluid ounces = 59 milliliters

$1/2$ cup = 8 tablespoons = 4 fluid ounces = 118 milliliters

1 cup = 16 tablespoons = 8 fluid ounces = 237 milliliters

1 pint = 2 cups = 16 fluid ounces = 473 milliliters

1 quart = 4 cups = 32 fluid ounces = 946 milliliters (.946 liter)

1 gallon = 4 quarts = 16 cups = 128 fluid ounces = 3.78 liters

1 ounce = 28 grams

$1/4$ pound = 4 ounces = 114 grams

1 pound = 16 ounces = 454 grams

2.2 pounds = 1,000 grams = 1 kilogram